HURRICANE WATCH NEW AND COLLECTED POEMS

Olive Senior is the Poet Laureate of Jamaica 2021–24. She is the award-winning author of twenty books of fiction, non-fiction, poetry and children's literature and other published work. Her many awards include Canada's Writers Trust Matt Cohen Award for Lifetime Achievement, the OCM Bocas Prize for Caribbean Literature, the Commonwealth Writers Prize, an honorary doctorate from the University of the West Indies and the Gold Medal of the Institute of Jamaica. Her work has been adapted for radio and stage, translated into many languages and is taught internationally. Olive Senior is from Jamaica and lives in Toronto, Canada, but returns frequently to the Caribbean which remains central to her work.

Olive Senior

Hurricane Watch

New and Collected Poems

CARCANET POETRY

First published in Great Britain in 2022 by
Carcanet
Alliance House, 30 Cross Street
Manchester, M2 7AQ
www.carcanet.co.uk

A CIP catalogue record for this book is
available from the British Library.

ISBN 978 1 80017 216 6

Book design by Andrew Latimer

The publisher acknowledges financial
assistance from Arts Council England.

Supported using public funding by
**ARTS COUNCIL
ENGLAND**

CONTENTS

SHELL (2007)

Gastropoda   15
Shell Out
   Hatch   19
   Maize   20
   Shelter   22
   Garden Snail   23
   Taíno Genesis   24
   Cassava/Yuca   26
   Skin   27
   Pearl   28
   The Skin of the Earth   29
   Sailor's Valentine   30
   Canoe Ocean   31
   Hurricanes   32
   Lucea Harbour   33
   The Song that it Sings   34
Shell Blow
   Shell Blow   39
   Send the Fool a Little Further   45
Shell Shock
   Quashie's Song   49
   Peppercorn   50
   Sweet   52
   Bwoy   52
   Cane Gang   55
   West India Cane Piece Rat (1821)   56
   Canefield Surprised by Emptiness   58
   Walking on Eggs   59
   What Could Be Written on a Grain of Rice   60
   Fishing in the Waters Where My Dreams Lie 61

At the Slavery Museum   63
Picture   64
Shelter
   Found Poem Regarding Archaeological Concerns   67
   Join-the-Dots   68
   Shell   70
   The First House   71
   S(h)ift   72
Empty Shell
   A Superficial Reading   77
   The Poetics of a West India Dinner Party   79
   Auction   81

OVER THE ROOFS OF THE WORLD (2005)
The Pull of Birds   91
1: *A Little Bird Told Me...*
   The Secret of Capturing Parrot   95
   The Secret of Taming Parrot   96
   The Secret of Turning Green Parrot Yellow   97
   The Secret of Flying Close to the Sun
      without Melting Wings   98
   The Secret of Crusoe's Parrot   100
   The Ultimate Secret   103
   Yard Fowl   104
   Hummingbird   107
   Woodpecker   108
   Parakeet   109
   Magpie   110
   Peacock Tale, 1   113
   Peacock Tale, 2   114
   Albatross   116
   Emperor Penguin   117
   Ostrich   118
   The Dance of Cranes   119

2. *Islanded*

   Allspice   123
   Discovery   124
   The Birth of Islands   125
   Message in a Bottle   126
   Thirteen Ways of Looking At Blackbird   127
   Misreading Wallace Stevens   130
   Rejected Text for a Tourist Brochure   133
   Missing   135
   Here And There   137
   Blue   138
   Leaving Home   140
   Lost Tropic   141
   Blue Magic Carpet   142
   Moon   144
   Wild Nester   145

3: *Penny Reel*

   With My Little Eye…   153
   Riddle   155
   Embroidery   156
   Penny Reel   158
   White   162
   Lacemaker   165
   Pearl Diver   167
   Basketmaker   169
   Bird-Man / Bird-Woman   170
   Ode To Pablo Neruda*   171

GARDENING IN THE TROPICS (1994)

Gourd   187

Travellers' Tales

   Meditation on Yellow   191
   Hurricane Story, 1903   199
   Moonshine Dolly   202

Hurricane Story, 1944   204
Cat's Cradle   208
Caribbean Basin Initiative   209
Hurricane Story, 1951   215
Illegal Immigrant   224
Stowaway   225
Meditation on Red   226
Hurricane Story, 1988   236
All Clear, 1928   238

Nature Studies
Plants   245
Starapple   247
Pineapple   248
Madam Fate   250
Fern   251
Mountain Pride   252
Sun and Moon   253
Snail   254
Guava   255
Guava/2   256
Guinep   257
Anatto and Guinep   258
Pawpaw   261
Bamboo (In Five Variations)   262

Gardening in the Tropics
Brief Lives   269
My Father's Blue Plantation   270
Finding Your Stone   272
The Knot Garden   273
The Colours of Birds   275
The Tree of Life   278
Seeing the Light   280
Amazon Women   283
Tropic Love   286

The Immovable Tenant   287
Gardening on the Run   293
Advice and Devices   298
Mystery
   Marassa: Divine Twins   305
   Obatala: Father of Wisdom   306
   Osanyin: God Of Herbalism   307
   Ososi: God of Hunting   308
   Ogun: God of Iron   309
   Shango: God of Thunder   311
   Orunmilla: God of Divination   314
   Babalu: Lord of the Earth   315
   Oya: Goddess of the Wind   317
   Olokun: God of the Deep Ocean   318
   Yemoja: Mother of Waters   321
   Guédé: Lord Of The Dead   324

TALKING OF TREES (1985)

Homescape   329
Birdshooting Season   330
Cockpit Country Dreams   331
Prayer   335
Drought   336
Ancestral Poem   337
To My Arawak Grandmother   339
Searching for Grandfather   340
Touchstone   342
Poltergeist   343
Hill Country   345
Eighth Birthday   347
Portrait   348
One Night, the Father   350
Childhood   352
Colonial Girls School   353

Nansi 'Tory   355
X   358
Nature Studies I   359
Nature Studies II   362
Epitaph   364
Revelation   365
Song of the Cave Valley Man   366
Song of the House   368
Funeral Song   369
Letter from the Lesser World   371
Cropover   374
Concrete City   376
Madman at Traffic Lights   377
To the Madwoman in My Yard   379
And What of the Headlines?   380
Apartment Life   382
Green Parakeets   384
Albert Street   385
r a i n   386
City Poem   388
The Scavenger   390
The Mother   391
The Lady   393
The Victim   395
The Dispatcher   396
Reaching My Station   399
Children's Hospital   402
Talking Of Trees   403

EYED: NEW AND UNCOLLECTED POEMS

Fabulous Eyelids   411
Eye Wash   412
Eye-Water   413
Eyelet/Aiglet   414
Out/In   415
Sure Shot   416
Killer Bees   417
White Night   418
Hurricane Watch   420
'Warning: Keep Away from the Cliffs'   421
Cruise Ship Leaving Port at Night   422
Dead Straight   423
Guava Jelly Score   425
Green Bush Green Bush Green Bush   426
Grand-Daughter Learns the Alphabet   428
Hook   429
They're Stoning the Mango Tree Again   430
Christmas Pudding   431
Country Funeral   432
Flight   433
Greenhorn   434
Persephone   435
The Drought   437
The Eye of Everything   440
Poem Without Ending...   445

Notes to the Poems   449
List of Illustrations   452
Index Of Poem Titles   453

SHELL (2007)

GASTROPODA

You think I've stayed home all my life,
moving at snail's pace, sneakily living off
another's labour? You think I've nought
to leave behind but empty shell? Come:
study me. Take my chambered shell apart.
Brace yourself for whirlwinds
coiled at my heart.

SHELL OUT

what if
i didn't want out
if happy in here floating
from one end to the other
in this wachamacallit   one day
opened just a peepshow   crack
jump back girl   back from the
sound of breaking blast from the
light let in   once lines get crossed
there's no turning back flood waters
sweep me through the hatch   hello
world   tap   crumbling walls
shell   out   set me up
for life
for breaking

MAIZE

'The first humans were created from corn.'
Popul Vuh, *Las antiguas historias del Quiché*

Mothers will understand this: The first ones I sent into the
world did alright, turned out to be human. But this lot!

Okay, perhaps I spoil them. Bearing them now not solitary
and naked like the first but many together, gift-wrapped

in silky down and swaddling clothes of papery layer.
I've overdone it, perhaps, in the way of security and

comfort. For can I get them to leave? Even when
mature they continue to cling for dear life to me and –

worse – to each other. Unwrapped, without the light of day,
they know they are useless but are still so shy, they are

prepared to die – together. To live, they must be forcibly
undressed and separated. That's where my human children

come in. Skilled at brutality, they will happily rip these
children from me, strip off their clothing, pull them apart.

Because I know it's for their own good, I watch as each little
one pops out like a pearl. Ivory. Golden. Milky.

Not all will stay that way. Some will be dried, popped,
parched, ground to be drunk or eaten. But I smile even as I

am myself cut down as spent and useless, for I know
enough of my progeny will be saved to be planted and

nurtured. Become, in their turn, mothers proudly displaying
their clinging children in their green array. The little ones

still attached to their mother, still clinging to one another;
undercover, in the dark. Scared of the single life. Yet

dying for exposure. To grow up. To ripen the germ
of Sun Father.

SHELTER

Growth rings inscribe
inside each shell
the markers of
a former life.

This shell, my skin,
outers a life
still stretched
still lived in.

GARDEN SNAIL

Snail locks up his mobile home for winter
pretends he's not at home
and goes to sleep.

For goodness' sake!
Who, when Spring comes
will tell him to awake? And how?

Who but the landlord of this trailer park
who dares to yell:
'Peel off and shell out. Now.'

TAÍNO GENESIS

We the people of Cacibajagua emerged
from the cave the moment Sun's longest leg
splintered the horizon. All went well except that
the sentry posted at the entrance at his first sight
of Sun blinked. Unwary sentinels cannot go
unpunished. With his eyes eclipsed who knows
what could have slipped through his grasp?
So Our Maker turned him into stone for his
tardiness and there he stands still: Macocael –
He-of-the-insomniac-eyes, our petrified eternal
guardian. We filed out expectantly, each one
trying not to cough and break the spell
as Sun's eye cracked open like guinep shell
and released us. We emerged dressed in our naked
best, not yet possessed of the feathers and beads
or the red anotto paint, the gift of Sun Father,
colour of worship and warrior, of
Hummingbird's iridescence. We would come
into the world stained black with our sacred
juice, guinep, colour of difficult passage
and tumescence. We would bleach in the sun
for nine days; then to the water to gather
the sacred herb *digo*, for the washing
to remove the last traces of our birth passage.
Guinep stain running like rain till
we reached again bare skin, our palette ready
for our first painting. Oh! Before
inscribing our names we should mention that
there was another cave, that of Amayauna –

the others, the people who do not matter
(to our story). We were Taíno, the ones gifted
with guinep or *jagua*. With sacred *bixa:* the herb
anatto. The ones shelled out by Sun Father.

CASSAVA/YUCA

When the Seven Sisters signal rain, the mothers make
ready: cradle cassava sticks for planting, like children in their
baskets.

To each they offer the incense of tobacco. Water with their
tears. Buried under each grave mound: their people's future
here.

> Radiate roots penetrate Mother Earth,
> douse for water. Children of Yuca
> shoot up high, fertilized by Sun Father.

In their gardens, the mothers softly tread, in dread lest they
awaken sleeping child of Yuca without reason. Pray
for the day the newly risen one cries out:

Cut me down. For you, I die each season. This is my body.
Come, dig me, peel me, grate me, squeeze me, dry me, sift
me, spread me, heat me.

Give me life again. Eat me.

SKIN

(After viewing Fernando Botero's work)

He's rumbled them, sketched them skin
stretched taut as drum.

Leaving flesh to make its ample statement
is so wise.

The rhythms of their stories freeze us
in black pearl eyes.

PEARL

Trophy wife, power object, your lustre fading
from neglect: Pull that rope from around your neck.

Don't you want to be free? Come now, break the spell.
Let each pearl be. Or cast them before swine. What

have you to lose? Honour, like the pearl, is already used.

Keep a single pearl for contemplation of the kingdom within,
or ingest it for melancholy, madness, and other

lunar folly. Better yet, count it a blessing, save for longevity.
Too many lives already lost for this string.

THE SKIN OF THE EARTH
(for Lyndal Osborne)

As startling in this gallery as pomander
of clove and orange, material from matter:
kelp, grass, stalk, stem, seed, and pith. All
return alive in the hands of the artist.
The essence not what we consume but what
remains and speaks to us across the room,
contained by its own weight as gesture, as
skeletal mountains of stalk, of skin.

So too we could lie, mountains of bones
beneath the skin of Earth that quietly
fashions our return. Not in that self-same
shell, that edifice of body, but encoded
in found matter like perfume
strong as clove, bittersweet as orange.
Tantalizing essence of what was once
the ripeness of ourselves.

SAILOR'S VALENTINE

Long after he is gone, a message
from a further shore arrives, the token
of a love alive. The wooden box
that sailors make for sweethearts
to display the lovingly collected
tribute shells in disingenuous array:

Helmets, false tritons, limpets, abalones,
whelks, olives, mitres, marginellas,
nutmeg and heart cockles....

On top, the message spells
in purple murex shells: 'Remember me'.

She gazes into the open box and feels imperilled, feels
the undertow of old wounds gaping, feels
the wavering before her eyes
          till she summons up the tearing that will cauterize,
that will flood the shells and speed them back her valentine
draining back to the grave, the empty sea.

C A N O E
O C E A N

permit me to skim your surface only my line
a little scratch my net a tickle my catch
like mites reaped from some great beast's hide

down deeper? o no thank you the drowned
gnaw songs of hunger in that kingdom underwater
swallow splinters of gnashed pride wondering
how did they transgress?

i will just humbly take a little fish here
and try not to upset

HURRICANES

Winds that are born out of thin air beyond the Gulf
bring other heartaches than hurricanes.

Hurricanes expose these empty shelves in our lives.

Did you know they were there before the winds
signalled us?

LUCEA HARBOUR

Importunate waves run ceaselessly to kiss the shore.
O rigid land, so indifferently receiving them.

so far from the sea I find myself
worldless. (Oh, leave it alone, but I meant
to write 'wordless.') And sometimes, like

tonight, I feel a hemispheric sadness: the
New World as tired as the rest. And there's
a waterlogged moon getting ready to burst

like the gourd that spilled an ocean when
the seeker, like myself, disobeyed, took it
down from where it hung by a thread,

dropped and broke it. So how were we
to know that from it seas would stream
forth, bringing three ships with our eclipse:

the Black Sun? Yet how but by disobedience
can we change the world order? So what if
all we are left with is a sieve to carry water?

We can use it to fish up a poem or two
to sail from our flagpoles. Or plant vines
to swim seeking radiate air, colonizing

the light to store it for rebirth: a summer
virgin in lace-mantle
of silver.

So excuse me for interjecting an ode here
to silver: to my vine of such magical growth,
and to moonlight, to starlight, to fish-scales,

to sighs, to sadness and whispers, to the pure light,
to water, to ripples over stone, to veils, to jewels
and cutlery, to tinsel, to glitter, to winners' cups

and chalices, to the lining of clouds, to watch cases,
to the instruments before steel, to erasures,
to anniversaries, to the snail's trail, to mother-

of-pearl, to musical notes that are liquid. To our
Earth seen from space, to the light of the fireflies,
to ice, to crystal – petrification of light,

to reflections of mirrors – the soul's shining.
To luminescence of eels, dust particles,
electricity. To anguish and the colour

of forgetting. To needles and pinpricks,
to the pure heart, the clear conscience,
the firm voice. To the keening that is never ending.

For the ocean is endless, the sea has no corners,
no turnings, no doors. And none can silence this song
that it sings.

SHELL BLOW

SHELL BLOW

I

Flesh is sweet but disposable, what counts
is shell. Like other objects beached, beyond
your ken, inert I lie, bleached and toneless

save for ocean song that only visitors claim
to hear. What if one day you accidentally
picked up the right shell – such as I; placed it

to your ear, pressed – by chance – the right
knob, there would pour out not the croak
of song soaked-up in sea-water and salt

but the real thing, a blast-out, everybody's
history: *areito, canto histórico*, a full
genealogy of this beach, this island people.

You could be blown away by what is held
custody here, every whorl a book of life,
a text, a motion picture, a recording,

or what passes for such in our island
version. You could begin anywhere.
Encoded in are full facilities for fast forward,

play, playback and dub, reversible though
not scrubbable. For we – as you know –
are master engineers when it comes to

scratching out a living on vinyl, on dutty
or plantation. We is Ginnal at the Controls!
Nansi Nation. We can rib it up, dibble it,

rub it, dub it and fracture it. Splice it. Spice
it up. But like a spite, we still can't find
a way to erase not one word. They say,

that is how History stay. Say you bound
to re-live it on and on. Unless you can find
a way to shell it out; pass it on.

PASS IT ON!

II

May we speak as I once did in tandem
with the old trumpet player, Shell-man
of the village who positioning me to his lips,

too-tooted out the notes to mark our
Angelus of work every day of the year?
Shell-blow for our mournings, our birthings,

to recount genealogies. For alarms
and warnings, for summons to meetings,
for connecting with the next hill.

Shell-man our bell-ringer, shell our telephone
to heaven and elsewhere. But I noticed
it got harder and harder for Shell-man

to blow notes that worth anything. People
no longer hearing, not wanting to listen
over the noise coming in. Harder for me

to give out when I couldn't take in
what was happening in our world. Heart
so full, nothing resounding. The emptiness

tunnelling the brains of the children,
noise of the cities trawling them in. Shell-man
lost and faded, castaway and toneless as shell.

III

O what tidings I could pour into the right ear,
perhaps yours? The real thing, what the
ordinary visitor would not hear. Every time

shell blow, we exhale another tale. Shall we
give it a whirl? So go on. What you waiting for?
Pick me up. Let us sit mouth to ear. Let me

put my tongue in, just for practice. There.
Are you scared? Do you find that thrilling?
Disturbing? Tintillating? Or simply wet?

Would you prefer to hear ocean roar? O
I can offer so much more than that old
croak soaked up in salt water, burning sand.

I want to woo you. Till you rue the day
you listened, for there's no turning back
till we get to the bottom of the rhythm:

too-toot of the conch, the funk of shak-shak.
By next shell-blow you blue and black.
For is head to head we have to go or if you

prefer toe to toe, wherever you have feeling
I am willing to go reeling off my song. For
it's too long I've been lying here forsaken –

since ol'time someting done weh – and I been
trying to reconnect to the centre of that whorl.
To have someone press that button, to say

HEY, MAN! LISSEN! IT'S THE DAMNDEST
THING! COME: PUT THIS SHELL TO YOUR
EAR. AS SURE AS HELL THERE'S

SOMETHING GOING ON IN HERE!

Say what?

PASS IT ON!

IV
Baby, I want you. I want to be your creature
of legend called Dry-head, the one once you
take it up you can never put it down. Unless

you find a way to pass it on. Like Burr-Lady,
Clinging-Woman, like the Rolling Head, Dry
Skull, that still be walking, talking, looking for

a way to reconnect with some living-breathing
body, and go hoist itself on top of you.
If your hand just pass over the button or you

eye-pass the page – just a glance or glancing
blow – know you taking up trouble, you
hoisting history on your back that I been trying

to download, to unload the years. So full
I stuff there's no space for the new.
Once shell stop blow is like time

stand still for people. As if they come into
the world just so. Been marking time
ever since. Convinced their name is Nobody,

born in a place that is called Nothing, for
it is Historyless. For History is invention
and nothing invent yaso according to

Famous Author that was the last
I was to hear about before all over
the Caribbean shell by any name stop blow:

kaachi, lambie, panchajanya, futoto.
And isn't it surreal that I'm stuffed so full
of history yet the only reel in my head is

that 'nothing/nothing' mantra that is like
that stone that got thrown down into
the Caribbean basin, rippling out to form

the arc of islands (so said other Famous
Author) then sinking, sinking into itself,
into *nada*?

For one who's been around as long as me
it's hard to bear; that's why I'm begging you
to lend me your ear. I will thank you,

praise song you. But beware! Once I grab you,
you can't do a thing, can never fling me off,
for the more you throw, the tighter I cling.

Better to relax. Listen and learn. No harm
ever come of that. Say: Yes, free paper burn.
Back to school again. Shell it out. Pop 'tory gimme.

First Lesson:
Faut al'la pou con la
'You must go there to know there'.
PASS IT ON!

SEND THE FOOL A LITTLE FURTHER

Likl bwoy, come here. Is April Fool Day. Tek this message to
that lady you see there. Do as she say. Make sure you don't
tek fas' open it up so read – I will know; I will give you bus'
ass! Plus you would find out it say: Send the fool a little
further. Heh-heh.

SHELL SHOCK

'The story of a lump of sugar is a whole lesson in political economy, in politics, and also in morality.'
Auguste Cochin, quoted in Manuel Moreno Fraginals,
The Sugar Mill

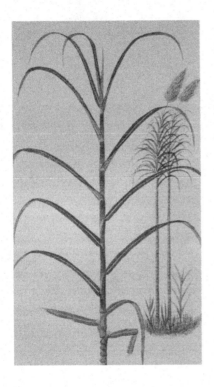

QUASHIE'S SONG

Here the John Crows wheel
And the whip keeps time
And the days dip by
And the sun keeps turning
And the seasons fly
And I'm old, old, in a flash.

When was I ever young?

PEPPERCORN

Torn from the vine in a place of moist
heat and shade where I was growing,
skin once plump and reddish, glowing.
Suddenly, a job lot. Indiscriminately
thrown in, we are jumbled, shaken up,
rolled together, little knowing our fate
or destination, till black and shrivelled
by the sun, looking all alike now, we are
tumbled into hold of a ship for forty days
and forty nights (we guess – for black
is the fenestration).

Disgorged, spilled out, shell-shocked
I come parched and dried, my head
emptied, till shock-still I come to rest,
shelled-out, buck-naked. In the mad
ensuing scramble, who will come
        who will come sample me,
view me, choose me, sort me out
for grade and quality, drive me home
to crush me, use me? Know that alone
I'm of little value, like a peppercorn
rental. All together, we can pepper
your arse with shot.

Over time, despite our treatment,
you'll see, survivors stay pungent
and hot. You can beat me senseless,
grind me down, crush me to bits, to
powder. You can never lose my bite
on your tongue, my hold on your senses:
forever I'll linger and cling.

In your mad scramble to possess,
devour me, remember, if you'd only
allow me to do a striptease, slow, peel off
my black skin, you'd be pleased –
or shocked – to discover: I'm white below.

SWEET
BWOY
Let's get just one thing
straight, right? Beneath this
fine, upstanding pose, this self-
contained exterior, I'm absolutely,
totally, in control. Sure, I'll let you
extract from me whatever you
desire – if you can pay the price.
So go ahead: grind me, juice me,
reduce me, fire me up, refine me,
till I yield what you want: this
shattered white crystal. Or – if
you like dark meat – this sticky
brown bag variety. I'm malleable.
I can crawl crude and slow like
molasses. I can also get spiritual,
transparent as rain, take you higher
with a kick that is deadly – I am
purest with age. Then I can
sweeten you, calm your rage.

I can't hide my origins; under-
neath, I'm raw and I'm crude,
I've a terrible reputation. Yea, I'm
brutal, a user of men, consumer of
acreage, the more virgin the better.
I love it when the forests burn to
prep the ground for me. When – just
to serve – millions are captured and
shipped across the sea. Okay, those
good old days are gone but slave

consumers – like you – are still born
every second. That's why I'm in the
driver's seat. I dictate the rhythm.
My seasons not spring, summer,
winter, but strictly rotated by
my needs: planting, reaping,
croptime. Then what they call
ha-ha! – the dead season.

For a brief spell, I give you
room. Recovering from excess,
I put down roots, send up shoots.
Each year, like a sickness I bloom.
For I'm the only one allowed to
flower. Fire my signature. I burn
human fuel. I dictate the rhythm
of the dance. I grow as tall as I
please, then do a slow striptease,
as armies move to chop me down.
But life is a battle-ground and I'll
always rise again. My recovery
quick, I come armed with the
weapons for battle: my razor-
sharp edges, my fuzz to work its
way under your skin. I choke
you with my lingering smell,
cover everywhere with my litter.

I can seduce young and old
with my upstanding demeanour,
pixilate them with my juice. Yes,
I'm the outsider, the interloper.
I've crossed the world to serve
you. I give you harvest: full belly.
An illusion. I sap the soil, end
fertility. I'll drive you to penury,
abandon you, move on. Yes, I'm
wild and I'm wicked. I'm arrogant.
I don't care. You'll find me every-
where. I don't discriminate. I'm
your foremost addiction. Your
kind will always treat me well. I
guarantee satisfaction.

CANE GANG

Torn from the vine from another world
to tame the wildness of the juice, assigned
with bill and hoe to field or factory, chained
by the voracious hunger of the sugar cane

the world's rapacious appetite for sweetness

How place names of my servitude mock me:
Eden, Golden Vale, Friendship, Green Valley,
Hermitage, Lethe, Retreat, Retirement, Content,
Paradise, Pheonix, Hope, Prospect, Providence

Each with the Great House squatting
on the highest eminence
the Sugar Works overlooking
my master's eye unyielding
the overseer unblinking
not seeing
the black specks
        floating across
                their finely-crafted
                        landscape

At shell blow assembled the broken-down
bodies, the job-lots scrambled into gangs
like beads on a string O not pearls no just
unmatched pairings the random bindings
like cane trash no not like the cane pieces
laid out geometric and given names
and burning.

WEST INDIA CANE PIECE RAT (1821)

What is lower than a rat?
I'm lower than that.

For Rat can climb, can wriggle and work its way out
of the trap. Rat can flap and jump to freedom.

What's better than that?

I sink to my knees in mud, rain or shine, weeding
the canefields, hoeing the line. Rat doesn't plant
but it reaps what's mine, or rather what's Massa's, for I
don't own a thing. While Rat is free, Massa owns me.

I'm lower than a rat.

Rat breeds as it likes, rat pikni never done.
Slave woman work like mule, we can't breed none.
And if we drop in our trace like Massa other beast,
he don't give a damn, plenty more where we come from.

What is worse than that?

The only thing I'm sure of as I hoe Massa cane

is that when Rat die, him not coming back again.
Not a soul going cry as Ratta turn back into dirt, as him
burn with the cane-trash, as him vanish from the earth.

Seh who better than Rat?
I better than that.

For I know that if I'm careful and I eat no salt.
If I don't mek Massa limb me, if I hold on to mi head
If I sing King Zambi song while I live in this here prison,
the minute that I'm dead, I fly straight back to Guinea.

What a day of rejoicing on that other shore, when the
nine nights are over and I'm home once more.
With the dead, with the living, with the children yet-to-be
in the bosom of my family I will once again be free.

So what you say now, Mister Rat?
What is better than that!

CANEFIELD SURPRISED BY EMPTINESS

It is not so much the shell shock as questions
we never asked that leave us cowering still
among the dead sugar metaphors.

Is this a legacy or something for which I am still
expected to pay? The circle on dust left by ghost
mules turning widdershins, turning the ghost
mills, turning the cane stalks into questions:

Are cane-cutters' children destined to rise,
like stalks, bloom like cane tassels, or to sink,
rootwise, into anger ratooning still?

Still as the closed circle of the mill.
Still as the knife blade descending.

This still life could wear us down.

WALKING ON EGGS

hanging
      on to

knowing
      not knowing

the contours of the minefield
      the trigger point
the charge

      knowing
not knowing

the reversals possible
      between madness
and cupidity
      extraction
and loaded gun
      between croptime
and planting
      fertility
and empty shell

I feel sometimes collected
      sometimes breakable

&
mindful

always
mind full of you.

Far from *Kun-Lun*
the crane's legs tied

I swallow the unfamiliar
with each breath.

Ku-li – bitter strength –
bound to sugar cane fields

to a circular season.
When my servitude ends

to mud I'll indenture.
Plant familiar green

seedlings yielding grain
hard as tropic.

Bitter strength
husking promise.

Futures written
on this grain:

the sight of
Kun Lun

FISHING IN THE WATERS WHERE MY DREAMS LIE

I

The day my master sent me fishing for his
      dinner
is the best day up to now I can remember.

This sea I found was not the sea that bound
      and swallowed me
that brought me hither, delivered me as less
      than what I left behind.
Here no looming seaside barracoons nor
      tattered sails nor the waves'
blue keening. What opened my eyes were
      the colours the sun
broke up on the water. Alone in my dugout
      shell, I dropped
my line and waited with baited breath,
      explored a vacancy
on my tongue. For here in this new world it is
      my master
who gives things names and here I am struck
      dumb, not knowing
how to summon them from the deep, what song
      to sing them
                so they'll leap.

O keepers of the deep release the catch or let
my master's vengeance fill this empty net.

By the powers of
Yemoja–Oboto
Agbe–Naete
Aizan–Velekete
Avrekete

Gede
Agoué
Olókun

II
I'm homing these waters
now I sing the joys of knowing
scales fall from my eyes hail
my brothers that swim from my
homeland to greet me here
clothed in the same bright dress
wearing new names

Each night I dream my net breaks up water
as water breaks up the shell-like image of the moon.

Praises I sing now to:

Agwé
Madre de Agua
Yemayá
Olókun

AT THE SLAVERY MUSEUM

The slave ship shell-shock dark
as the night-filled gourd

Cavernous as a grave fault

The viewer's mind
stretches to fit.
Fails to grasp

              until

we come to it

the child's body flexed
not yet shelled out.

At the heart of this search
something breaks.

Outside: the Sun has his eye on

the truth that spirals out of ( )hell.

PICTURE

We who fear exposure most are cursed
with eyes demanding wholeness. Not
what the painter sees: the charming,
lying version, the picturesque. O no.
Not like that here. This retina assembles
fractured images only, repairs the shattered
pieces. Trawls for evidence in shadowed
light, traces fleeting fragments in ghostly
black and white. The impetus: to close
the circle, to seek transparency, to open
the shutter wide
               to hold it steady. Receive
the measured quantity of light.

Snap!

            this incarnate, wholesome, image.

SHELTER

FOUND POEM REGARDING ARCHAEOLOGICAL CONCERNS

Broken and fragmented material
recovered through excavation

quantifiable

patterns observable in the frequency and
distribution of discarded

goods

JOIN-THE-DOTS

*'In the sample of 282 plantation maps drawn from the
National Library of Jamaica's collection, some 25 per cent
show the "village" area as a blank.'*
Barry Higman, *Jamaica Surveyed*

We played at Join-the-Dots, Grandma and me,
but never could we win the prize.
For I saw pictures she could not see,
They said I had clear-seeing eyes.

Our house was built on land where once
a village stood. Where fragments
floating in the air sometimes cried out
for personhood.

They pounded on the rooftop, tore at
the gutter. 'Hush, it is the wind,'
Grandma said, but I knew better
though I would never

utter a word. For I was sworn to secrets.
'This is where we once lived too,'
the children said. 'We'd like
to play with you.'

When I could not sleep for black dots
floating, Grandma said, 'Hush,
I'll bring you cocoa-tea sweetened
with cane sugar and

a hint of nutmeg. That will calm you
down.' I'd try to share it with my
ghostly friends who said they
lived in land-snail shells

and sailed all night the village round.
Their Old One said: 'No. You drink up,
child. For this our bodies
turned to dust. Ground

into fields of sugar cane, of cocoa-walks,
of nutmeg groves. Drink.
In remembrance of us.'
I'd drain the cup.

The cocoa, cane sugar, the nutmeg, touched me
so sweetly, I'd sleep long. Sleep deeply.

SHELL

From the Great House shell, we salvage bricks,
we pick up sticks, we never throw away.
We use things up as we are used. What can we
leave to speak of us?
            We do not eat off sets of plate or dine
in state or even sit at table. Our fragile artefacts
a yabba, monkey jar, our calabashes, mortar,
a cast-iron pot (from massa's store), a grinding
stone. These alone with our firestick, our
kreng-kreng basket, our three smooth firestones
form our domestic hearth, our altar.

So if in years to come some people
might be mad enough to search for us,
to trace our passing, they would have
to dig deep to find us here, sift ashes,
measure bones and beads and shell discarded.
            Just as the men long ago
digging the foundations of the Great House
my grandfather did say, came across fragments
of the true landowners, the ones before us,
the ones whose bones they buried under fill.
The 'Indian' people that once possessed it,

and possess us still.

THE FIRST HOUSE

Homeless, Deminán and his brothers,
orphaned and wandering forefathers,
Winds of Four Quarters, blew hither
and yon until

       Turtle-Woman stopped them
in their tracks: the first mating. Said:
I am ready for nesting. Said: Build me
a house. Untrained, but undaunted
(in the way of such heroes) they each
took a corner of the world, stood like
pillars to anchor it, and strained and
puffed to lift high the roof of sky,
which billowed out and in (they had
a hell of a time controlling it) until
it righted itself and domed into
the model of Turtle-Woman's shell.

And so we were born in the House
of our Great Mother, our crabbed
and comforting genitor, who still bears
our first house on her back.

S(H)IFT

I

Dig

here

sift and measure and
keep on miss
          ing me

                    there
on pathways
unrecorded
ephemeral
as snail trail
ing silver un
der fences by
passing bound
aries evad
ing cartography

here
          picture me
          as background fill
          black dots inch
          ing stead
          ily for
          ward
          to fill –

ah
you blinked

missed
> the pathways of the lash
> inscribed on my back
> the calligraphy of burning
> on my fettered wrists

missed
the place where I house a knot
where memory thickens and pearls.

II

Sift

our fragile fetishes of power:
eggshell, feather, powdered horn,
grave dirt and endurance.
> Shift –

Yes
I invested in dress, in adornment.
A life too short for the weight of
accumulation
> for provision
beyond
this
very sunset

When I'll be

born again
born again

my soul hidden
in shell

spiralling
down to clear water
to the valleys of the sea
where the turquoise bleeds into indigo
entrapping eternity.

William Beckford Jr., called by Lord Byron 'England's richest son', never once saw the source of his wealth.

In March 1787 he boarded a ship in England to visit his Jamaican plantations but got off at the first stop, Lisbon. He wrote in a letter: 'The more I hear of Jamaica, the more I dread the climate, which I fully expect will wither my health away… you must excuse my going any further…'

When Beckford died (at Bath in 1844) The Times *described him as 'One of the very few possessors of great wealth who have honestly tried to spend it poetically.'*

A SUPERFICIAL READING

*(An eighteenth century painting of the titled English lady
and her black child slave)*

Turn the page and revel in the surface opulence
of moiré silk, of creamware, pearlware, skin.
The shell-like ear behind the torque of ringlets,

the black pearl eyes. The pose is classical.
She does not really notice you within the triangle
of her body and embracing arm not sheltering,

more like cold marble. You kneel and the painter
collapses your upper body into a sign:
a small black triangle. Her touch is light for you

are a page she cannot read or write on. You are
an accessory to fashion, like the pearl choker
loaned you for the occasion which collars you

and separates your head from your body
(reminding you of an earlier truncation.) There is
no mind over matter for you are owned. You

exist merely to make her seem more luminous.
She does not know that perfection is shadowed
always, like a phantom limb. She does not know

about inversion and that the right hand never
shows what the left is doing. So that your prop,
that fake offering of shell like Pandora's box

could spill and pearl her skin like a sickness,
bloom like stigmata with no Erzulie here
to plead for her, no Santiago de Compostela

to intercede. She does not know you are
the Sable Venus-in-waiting, the black pearl
poised to be borne on cusp of emptied shell.

THE POETICS OF A WEST INDIA DINNER PARTY
(mid-seventeenth century) *

First then (because beefe being the greatest rarity in the Island,
especially such as this is) I will begin with it,
and of that sort there are these dishes at either messe,
a Rumpe boyl'd,
a Chine roasted,
a large piece of the brest roasted, the Cheeks bak'd, of which is a
      dish to either messe,
the tongue and part of the tripes minc'd for Pyes, season'd with
      sweet Herbs finely minc'd, suet, Spice, and currans;
the legges, pallets and other ingredients for an Olio Podrido
to either messe, a dish of Marrow-bones,
so here are 14 dishes at the Table and all of beefe;
and this he intends as the great Regalio, to which he invites
      his fellow planters; who having well eaten of it,
      the dishes are taken away,

and another Course brought in, which is
a Potato pudding,
a dish of Scots collips of a legge of Porke, as good as any in the
      world,
a fricasy of the same,
a dish of boyl'd Chickens,
a shoulder of younge Goate drest with his blood and tyme,
a Kid with a pudding in his belly,
a sucking Pig, which is there the fattest whitest and sweetest in
      the world, with the fragrant sauce of the brains, salt, sage
      and Nutmeg done with Claret wine,
a shoulder of Mutton which is there a rare dish,
a Pasty of the side of a young Goate, and a side of a fat young
      Shot upon it, well season'd with Pepper and salt, and with
      some Nutmeg,

---

* *Taken, word for word (and arranged 'poetically') from Richard Ligon,*
A True and Exact Account of the Island of Barbados *(London, 1657)*   **79**

a loyne of Veale, to which there wants no sauce being so well
      finisht with Oranges, Lymons, and Lymes,
three young Turkies in a dish,
two Capons, of which sort I have seen some extreme large and
      very fat,
two henns with eggs in a dish,
four Ducklings, eight Turtle Doves and three Rabbets;
and for cold bak'd meats,
two Muskovie Ducks larded, and seasoned well with pepper and
      salt;
and these being taken off the Table,

another course is set on, and that is
of Westphalia or Spanish bacon,
dried Neats Tongues,
Botargo,
pickled Oysters,
Caviare,
Anchovies,
Olives and (intermixt with these) Custards, Creams, some alone,
      some with preserves of Plantines, Banana, Guavers, put
      in, and those preserv'd alone by themselves,
Cheese-cakes,
Puffes, which are to be made with English flower, and bread, for
      the Cassavie will not serve for this kind of cookerie;
sometimes Tansies, sometimes Froizes or Amulets, and for fruite,
      Plantines, Bananoes, Guavers, Milions, prickled Peare,
      Anchove Peare, Prickled Apple, Custard Apple, water
      Milions, and Pines worth all that went before.
To this meat you seldom faile of this drink, Mobbie, Beveridge,
      Brandy, Kill-Divell, Drink of the Plantine, Claret wine,
      White wine, and Renish wine, Sherry, Canary, Red sack,
      wine of the Fiall, with all spirits that come from England.

AUCTION

I

The poetics of men who rose from nothing but auctions
from slave-ships, from piracy and smuggling, who pulled

themselves up by the canestalk, ratooned rich as eastern po-
tentates, retiring to England to don the furs and golden

chains of office, to embed themselves at the heart of its
civic institutions, its rotten boroughs, the only place to feel

at home in. Buying their way into society, ennobling
their progeny. Nesting like exotic species around London's

Georgian squares. Till, sickened by memory, haunted
by the smell of burning canefields, of boiling sugar,

molasses, rum, bagasse, of blackened sweated labour,
dying of ostentation, they retire, ill and over-fed, to Bath,

'to sucke in some of the sweet ayre of England,' to expire,
leaving behind a spurious genealogy. Erased the ignoble

birth, the slackness, any hint of blackness, save on the page,
the black boy as accessory with silver dog collar, dressed

and possessed as adornment to highlight wealth,
to heighten whiteness. To iconize imperial distance.

And at the 'plundering frontiers of Empire,'
the powerful father, who built his own oriental
palace, his Egyptian Hall, who sired English

bastards, on whose death Chatterton wrote
an ode, who hired the nine-year-old Mozart
to teach his infant son musical composition,

rich and powerful enough to publicly call
the English nobility subalterns to the body of
the nation. And yet to his Lord Mayor's banquet

they come, 600 dishes served on gold plate.
In attendance: 6 Dukes, 2 Marquises, 23 Earls,
4 Viscounts, 14 Barons and 18 Baronets.

His legitimate heir destined to become
England's richest son. Yet after all that gilded
promise, so despised, so alone, so shunned.

O what can fill this emptiness?

III

Taste and beauty over-cultivated.
The planter planting the Rose Garden,
Thornery, Pinetum, the Alpine Garden –
epitome of the sublime, the picturesque.

At auction, books and paintings bought and sold
in lots
      like slaves
            fondled

as my master in far-off England
                        fondles
the rare book he purchases, examines
for age and shape, hefts for weight,
caresses for surface scratches, tests
the latches
      the hide toughened
like the leather bindings
my master unties
                 cuts
the bound sheets to view the inside and finds
the white pages covered O
covered with such tiny black fragments.

O my word!
My master takes home the latest acquisition
for his collection, borne by six footmen in
gold and embroidery. Alone, the man on whom
no neighbours would call enters his barbaric
high tower furnished in gold, crimson, scarlet,
purple and ebony. Alone, he sits to decipher
the black markings, his feet propped upon
an antique footstool: a kneeling blackamoor

To find
        each letter, ant-like, running together
in a black connecting trail. A coffle. A sentence.

My master reads in silence. Alone. A cypher in a
hollow nest.

O what can fill this emptiness?

IV

What but the poetics of possessions, enough
to make the visitor 'dazzled and drunk with beauty'

        Greek vases of chalcedonian onyx
        Sevres china
        Egyptian porphyry
        Cabinet by Bernini
        Madame de Pompadour's black lacquer box
        Buhl armoires from the Louvre palace
        Ormolu chandeliers
        Mosaic tables of Florentine marble
        Persian carpets
        and
        Portrait of de Vos of Grotius
        Portrait of Rembrandt painted by himself
        Portrait of Pope Gregory, by Passerotti
        Portrait of Cosmo de Medici by Bronzino Allori
            ('fresh as if painted yesterday')
        and
        rusty helmets
        tattered shields
        inscriptions and broken milestones

medals
tessellated pavements
shiploads of mutilated figures
holy fragments
pagan images
and
'purchases made in the teeth of the Holy Roman
          Emporer and the King of France'
        at the Duc de la Valiere's sale of the century.

v

Not here
not here to disfigure the aesthetics, to mar
the poetics of Fonthill Tower, but locked in
the office of his London agent, his sugar factor,
the artefacts of high finance: beautifully engraved
Bills of Exchange.

Not here
the tedium of the counting house, the utter
boredom of grinding out so much money.

Not here
not here to sully the perfection
of the picturesque but under a vertical sun and
the eye of the nigger-driver,
        hopping to it on his Jamaican plantations,
to turn the wheels that spin the green-cane into
gold-
        en sugar crystals
            tripping
                    to a different poetic meter

                              to prime the
                    pumps
of a new technology,
            the industrial
                    revolution
                         in far-off England:
                                    600 beautifully
                                    scarred and
                                    artistically
                                    mutilated
                                    black slaves.

VI

Here
no black page but a Swiss dwarf
and hundreds of volumes in choice old Morocco
bindings.

VII

To house it all the neo-Gothic Tower at Fonthill
aimed at eliciting sentiments of amazement,
shock and awe built in record time by my
master whom they called a 'nigger-driver' not
referring to his progenitor but for the way he
drove architects builders contractors gardeners
to complete in speed the 'Grand Babel' the
enchanted gardens and monastic demense
locked within a wall twelve feet high and seven
miles long and gated,
            encircling 500 acres of a

'contrived, flowering wilderness' and Gothic
sham ruins.

If he had waited, in no time at all the ruin would
have become all too real. When the tower came
crashing down, he had already sealed a deal and
sold it.

VIII

How time and distance swallow the vanished
ruins, the mock glens and pastures, wild copse
and groves of pine. How the Wiltshire Downs
reclaim the artificiality of the picturesque.

Nothing remaining of vanished pride and tower
except the possessions auctioned, collected in
other citadels of power: libraries, museums,
galleries, castles, to gather dust in other empty

rooms where consumers still consume in
loneliness. Day after day, in gilded halls, the
servant armies vacuum, and wonder: Whence
comes this dust?
                O could it have been when
you introduced into your aristocratic domains,
for style and decorative effect, those black
pages?

Our fragile fetishes of power, our powdered
fragments, rise now to lightly dust these precious
artefacts, these hollowed shelves. And nothing
can stave off the relentless grinding down by

this new slavery: the collections, the recordings, the writing of history. And none can shackle passing time that is excavating from within, the promise of the silenced voices: the resonance of emptied shell.

OVER THE ROOFS OF THE WORLD (2005)

'I too am not a bit tamed, I too am untranslatable,
I sound my barbaric yawp over the roofs of the world.'

Walt Whitman, *Song of Myself*

THE PULL OF BIRDS

Colón, son and grand-son of weavers
    rejected that calling but did not
        neglect craft (keeping two sets of books).
      On his first voyage, landfall receding
        (where was Japan?) he sailed on

    praying for a miracle to centre him
      in that unmarked immensity, as warp to woof.
      And suddenly from the north a density
        of birds flying south, their autumn migration
        intersecting his westward passage.

  At such an auspicious conjunction, his charts
    he threw out, the flocks drew him south
    across the blue fabric of the Atlantic.
    Weary mariners buoyed by the miracle
        of land soon, of birds flying across the moon.

Birds seeking to outdistance three raptors skimming
        the surface of the sea and sending skyward
        their doomsday utterance of hawks' bells
          tinkling endlessly. Birds speeding
            to make landfall at Guanahaní.

1: A LITTLE BIRD TOLD ME...

THE SECRET OF CAPTURING PARROT

Up in the tree, wild Parrot sinks into the green canopy
and mimics silence. Speech comes only when spoken to.
His captors use smoke to draw him in: pimento wood and
resin on a fire built under the tree Parrot is perched in.
They'll sit and wait till Parrot is stunned enough to drop.

How will they know where Parrot is hiding?

The wind shifts.
        Parrot's captors break out in a fit of coughing.

                Coughing
                        unleashes
                                Parrot's tongue.

Wild Parrot can be tamed
   By gently blowing
      Tobacco smoke
         Over its beak
            And laughing.

THE SECRET OF TURNING GREEN PARROT YELLOW

The secret of that outward transformation
    comes
        from within.

Defeathered and rubbed with Toad's blood,
    Green Parrot
        grows new feathers

of a red or yellow hue.
    (Others claim that making Parrot eat the fat
        of certain fish will do.)

Humans use Parrot feathers
    to transform themselves
        from the outside in.

But what does Toad have to say? Was it millennia of hope
that evolved its blood as the perfect medium for heightening
Parrot's display? Or were the blood ties always there? Have
amphibia been harbouring a secret desire for uplift ever since
they watched their bird cousins soar away? Does Toad hope
Parrot will one day leak the secret of flight, of speech,
of colour, to its blood?

THE SECRET OF FLYING CLOSE TO THE SUN
WITHOUT MELTING WINGS

Discard the illusion of bearing yourself up. Only Bird,
    Sun's messenger, can transport you. This is not
        about wings of power

(that will burn, melt) but the power of wings lent to you
    by Grandfather Macaw. *If* he chooses
        to hear you.

Know that you come into the world featherless
    and naked. Like an egg. A cypher.
        Grandfather might permit you to pluck

one set of feathers to dress yourself in. Lend you hollow
    bones (to be returned after flight); breathe you into
        the lightness of air. (The feathers you might

be allowed to keep for many lifetimes). To prepare, know
    it is not a question of artifice but of becoming.
        Not build up but strip down. To dress up

you need the feathers, the paint, the beads, the flowers.
    The hallucinogenic rhythm of the rattles, the
        drums, your steed.

Power will come not swiftly on the wing but feather out of
    the homage. The humility. The loving
        preparation. The desire

to transform into Other. Leading to that auspicious moment:
    the whirr of wings speak plain. You have entered
        that place where flight is a given.

For you, flight is given as gift of bird messenger sustained
by rattle, by drum, by song. You soar, sail, glide.
For a brief moment you gain Sun's nod.

You are Bird itself. But know: such ecstasy is not forever.
You will re-enter your world, but let down lightly
cradled as gently as egg.

THE SECRET OF CRUSOE'S PARROT

Parrot through heavily-lidded eyes, watches as the new
     invader arrives. Friend or foe? Parrot doesn't know,
          doesn't care. Parrot is ruler of air.

This island kingdom was Parrot's from time immemorial,
     before arrivals, departures, of many such as he.
          Their claims of overlordship

as predictable as the tide. Parrot's weakness is that he
     loves company; even a human will do.
          Parrot is all pretence, mimicry,

playing fool to catch wise. Yet if Crusoe had asked, Parrot
     would have told no lies; he'd seen it all before.
          Could have told where the fresh springs were;

how to bake bread, set traps, fire pottery. Where best
     to build the boat. But (Parrot thinks) I mustn't gloat
          for then I would have deprived

the poor creature of his illusion of mastery, and myself
     of some good jokes. Such as his thinking
          I'm alone and celibate. *Poor Poll*

says he. *You are just like me.* Not knowing what lurks
     disguised as sweet juicy fruit in yonder tree –
          My mate. My progeny.

I let him teach me speech for much I forget between
visitors. And granted that such speech as I usually
imbibe – from cannibals, pirates,

buccaneers, delirious castaways, is not appropriate
for his Christian ears. Though sometimes
when I'm angry or for mischief

I let fly a few. He usually attributes these to his loneliness
and delirium; or to his mishearing. He prays
extra hard those nights.

'Poor Robin Crusoe,' I mock him. 'Where have you been?
How come you here?' *Poll*, he claims loftily, *the
only person permitted to talk to me.*

His servant, indeed. When that other creature came, the
one called Friday, I almost left him (that one was
a quick study. Knew exactly how

to please). I stayed because being 'Crusoe's parrot' does
give me status among the poor dumb creatures
in the trees. Now their teacher is me.

I had thought of peopling the island with educated parrots
and sweet airs. But I laid off the teaching
when I found I could no longer stand

their screeching. Since he arrived, my hearing is not what
it used to be. I find the senseless cries of those
uncivilized birds unbearable – as they find

talkative me. Once he goes, I'll have to find my place again
among my own, go back to playing dumb. Knowing
I cannot stave off the yearning

that will master me for words addictive as grain cracked open
on the tongue. Ashamed, alone again,
I'll start to haunt the beach, waiting for

another to come along, to gift me speech.

It wasn't after all Snake's tongue but Parrot in disguise.
The hint contained in its whispered cries: *Eve: Eva: Ave.*

YARD FOWL

Rooster

As long as a Rooster somewhere
is angry enough to claw at
the sun blood red rising and
pull it through, day will come:
the world will go on.

Hen

*'Woman luck lie a dungle heap, fowl
come scratch it up.'*
Jamaican saying

Some find you loud mouth and simple,
for every egg laid a big announcement
        a cackle, some find you
the broody hen, not knowing all
is meant to throw spies off the scent
of your blood's secret: you know
the sky isn't falling, geese don't lay
golden eggs, superior knowledge
resides in the feet.

You are mistress of maps to the under
layer, to buried treasure. Why else
do you nod your head and give thanks
as you sup? With every scratch,
woman's luck you turn up.

Senseh

O for a peel-neck hen, one with
            ruffled feathers, magic in its feet
                        to scratch up conjuration.
Defeat
            the enemy.
                        One to signal where

the danger lies, so we can root it out
            make fresh breeze blow, allow
                        the children to grow.

Ol'people say, every yard must have
a senseh fowl to brings things
into the open, make the wicked pay,
give the people the courage
to try out each new day.

Guinea Hen

In Granny's eyes, our foremost barnyard warrior is not
            after all our fierce Rooster or surly Turkey Gobbler
but mild Guinea Hen, her badge of office her spotted
            feathers. She stands on guard at that barrier they call
Reputation. For Granny explicating the difference
            between Good Girls and Bad always ends her homily
with warning as fact: *Seven year not enough*
            to wash speckle off Guinea Hen back.

When Granny holds up Guinea Hen as the symbol
of spoilt reputation, we study her pattern and interpret
Granny's warning to mean: *Not that you can't do so.*
            Just don't let the world know.
            Never let the spots show.

Owl

'the Owl was a baker's daughter'
Hamlet, IV: 5

Owl isn't a yard dweller though it lives in close proximity,
overlooking house and land from its niche
in the breadfruit tree.

I hardly ever see it. Its presence I sense when the air
seems churned into motion at dusk; a pricking
of the skin signalling

the ghostly hunter on the wing. The world seems shaken
to feel Owl measure out the air into quadrants
for better stalking; sift the night for prey.

To the old people Owl is ill-favoured, rider of nightmares
like half-baked dreams sprinkled
with grave dust.

So why do I on some days awaken to a ghostly presence
which does not leave me with dread
but a half-life

of something soothing and warm-scented, a present of
morning's rising crust:
the fecundity of bread.

HUMMINGBIRD

Your daily stance your warrior pose
against the Sun to vanquish foes.
Your virility glows. For your capoeira
dance, the drum rolls beaten by your heart.

When Sun retires, you too withdraw.

Your heart surprised at sudden rest
can leave you life-less.

Should this be death, you know
you'll rise again on beat of wings
reborn as bird, iridescent dazzler.
But still the warrior that never rests

till day is done, for Sun's the same

and will require your glowing ardour
to light his flame.

Forever combat-ready, dancing now
before the flowers of fire, lancing
the hearts you claim as your
domain: their hidden cache

the elixir of immortality, the honey

reserved for warriors of
Blue-Hummingbird-of-the-Left:
Huitzilopochtli.

WOODPECKER

'Women were created from yellow-skin plum trees
transformed by the action of the woodpecker.'
Amerindian myth

O Miss Yellow-skin Plum, Miss Prune-face,
Miss Disdainful One. Rejecting all suitors.
Still waiting for that magnificent descent
of Woodpeckers!

But times have changed, nuh? So wait on
for the eternally absent, the incomparably
selfish one. Or heed Woodpecker's song,
that barb-tipped tongue:

Plum-tree woman, O my dumb one,
Your secret still sweet as when locked up tight.
My pecker's eternal drumming I cannot disguise,
My need so intense, my greed so unsatisfied,
Perversity my preference now: dead-wood
To wooden bride.

No virgins anymore anywhere.
Woodpecker doesn't care.
He's got what he wanted:
His bright red hair.

O Miss Yellow-skin Plum, Miss Prune-face,
Miss Disdainful One, Miss Wait-a-Bit,
You hear that? You'd better start
transforming yourself.

PARAKEET

'I heard a parakeet in the garden
he was talking to Jesus alone
It was Judas betraying the master…'
Jamaican Revival hymn

No longer do we find amusing your surface disguise
as fig- or bulletwood-leaf, as red-peas pod, as unripe mango,
as milk-corn cob. We have learnt how childish chatter can
obscure sinister intention, gregariousness mask selfishness,
mischievousness disguise cunning.

Rejecting flesh, you savage pimento to devour the seeds;
slice into orange for its pips, tear cashew to bits for its kernel.
Nothing is sacred. Yet we have learnt parrot-fashion from
you, a thing or two: how to attack the surface over and over
till we rip it apart, enabling us to reach the entrails, expose
the tatters of this masquerade, this pitchy-patchy Perroquet.
Perroque. Pierrot. Pierre.

Revealing, not Peter, but a Judas here.

Couldn't you even try to be as easy as neat
as buttoned up as pie with its secrets under cover

no revealing what's concealed till invited? No
spilling out and blabbing to the world (not even

a whisper of four-and-twenty blackbirds baked in –
not before they're summoned to sing). O Magpie,

can't you learn from the very concoction
you've given name to, its lush inside as mixed-up,

as pied as you are, but such tight control, such
a buttoned-down and crusty exterior!

Can't you see how like type out of wack, all pied up,
you gabble words that are senseless? If only

you'd stop and swallow a few before speaking. But no!
Take that back, we shouldn't mention 'swallow'

in your hearing, since your name – 'pica' – has been given
by the medical profession to that obsession with eating

unsuitable objects, such as chalk, clay, or – by those
in that so-called 'delicate way' – pied choices like

green eggs and ham, or chocolate and jelly with lamb
(or anything else that will rhyme in the belly).

You've been accused of 'conspicuous arrogance', greed,
gossip, dissipation, vanity – Bacchus your lord, symbol

of drunkenness and garrulity; of engaging in
'indiscriminate collection' – known as thievery. Even

your name you have plucked from the tongues of
chattering women (also 'pied'); O the poor little

Margaret now forced to be Mag (and fit to be tied!).
You've also been identified with poets though

I myself the connection cannot divine except
perhaps through Bacchus – and a few drops of wine?

Though you might also have been that folk poet
back then, the Pied Piper, that made off

with the children when – imagine the irony –
you're the one who could say on this solitary

occasion: "I wuz robbed." Your reputation needs
rescuing but you make it so hard as I find you

parading in yard after yard in our neighbourhood,
sitting on fences, teasing the dogs, engaging in

seemingly senseless chatter – to divert from
what you plan to nick.

Plus, I do hate talebearers and I've just heard
this trick: that once upon a time when

a couple had to be parted for a while, each
gave the other a mirror. Should one be unfaithful,

that mirror would change instantly into you, Magpie,
and you'd fly straight back to the other – with the news.

O why did I choose to defend such a blabbermouth?
But you simply refuse to be overlooked, you

celebrant of the variegated, the parti-coloured,
mixture of paint, pigment, picture of pied beauty.

For I too am pied. And no one has ever said you've lied.
No hypocrite you, I can relate to that.

No struggle to figure you out. It's obvious as black
and white. Plain as night and day. Easy as pie.

PEACOCK TALE, 1

Once upon a time, Peacocks were eaten
        but only by Royalty and therein
                hangs a tale.
King George the Third in a moment of
        lucidity, was set to practicing
                his Speech from the Throne.
All went well, except that at the end of
        every sentence he intoned
                the word: 'Peacock'.
The Minister sent to drill him scratched
        his head and finally said:
                "Majesty, 'peacock'
is a very fine word. So fine indeed it
        needs be reserved exclusively
                for Royalty. If you pardon me
– Majesty – such a word should never
        be breathed aloud to excite
                the common herd."
This pleased the king excessively.
        Thereafter his speech he said
                punctuated by the word
'peacock' but silently at the end
        of every sentence. Interpreted
                as a strategic pause
which many said made for an excellent
        delivery. Still, some kept muttering
                'insane'. Not knowing
that in eating peacock, the King
        had swallowed not just bird
                but word.

Which is to say, with the goose: sauce.
With the peacock: sorcery.

The navy from Tarshish arrives with gold and silver,
ivory, apes, and Peacock, with his hundred eyes.

King Solomon brings his children and his hundred wives.
Stretching a mile or so long, they line up on the wharf

to view the strange barbaric throng. Peacock assumes
the reception is for him and almost manages a song.

Peahen, ignored by everyone, dutifully following in his
rhythm, carries the suitcases and a flagon of

smelling salts. Peacock marches up and down and struts
his stuff and preens. Until he fluffs his tail and careens

to the limit of his pride. It is then that Peahen rushes
to his side and hisses in her quiet voice: "Feet! Feet!"

Peacock, as if stung, whimpers and in retreat lowers
his head in shame. Pride falls like his eyes to the ground

and his ugly black feet. Peahen unstoppers the smelling
salts and delivers it neat. Peahen does not consider

herself cruel, or, as some would have it, consumed by
jealousy. Oh no, she says, it's just that a woman's got to

protect the one who puts bread on the table, even from
himself. Nobody looking at him (she says) would suppose

his brain to be the size of a pea, his head so light, all that
arrests his fancy, or even more permanent flight is his

wife – me – having to remind him every time, of those ugly
black feet. The only thing that keeps him grounded – and in line.

ALBATROSS

Long before Copernicus or Galileo
the Albatross had taken the Earth's measure,
surveyed its daily round. It chose the life of
the outsider, putting its trust in the ribbon of winds
girdling the world. Once airborne, the Albatross
turns stateless ocean rover, its impetus born
of knowing that in going forward it will always
be homing back.

EMPEROR PENGUIN

The Emperor Penguin stands sentinel to progeny in the dark
Antarctic winter. Two months solitary on the Great Ice Barrier
incubating a single egg in the fold of the skin between his legs.
By the time his mate returns from her long eating spell
to relieve him, he's but a shadow of his former self.
Such parental cooperation! Sounds to me like a marriage made
in Hell. Penguins perhaps are too well matched. By the time
mating season draws near, the male has forgotten all he's
learnt the previous year. With everyone dressing unisex,
he sometimes presses the wrong suit. The consequences could
be appalling. What does an Emperor Penguin do with no egg
to hatch on the Great Ice Barrier during the dark Antarctic
winter? It seems as if in exchanging wings for flippers, flight
for fortitude, the courageous Emperor Penguin made a mess of dress.

OSTRICH

Ostrich in forsaking flight for speed, gave up
the empowerment of challenging gravity.
Slick and swift as a steed, its feet are also
weapons: Ostrich can turn vicious.

In choosing Earth, did Ostrich abandon
that loop connecting worlds to indulge
its own base instinct? Or is fight to earth
the natural pair, as flight to Air?

THE DANCE OF CRANES

Ancient priestesses schooled
    in dance notation
        copied down the mating
dance of cranes to use as blueprints
    for constructing
        labyrinths
so initiates might wind their way to ecstasy.

Cranes
        whose
                ful
            joy
    intricate
      dances

            sum
        moned
the   spring

    to distant places
        cranes
           whose   flight

confounded

   distances
        and elemental

            spaces.

Imagine such distance   wound into
such small compass.   The ecstatic
twists and turns   the joyful   leaps
contorted.   The   magic   of   the
flight   of cranes   reduced   to an
earthbound   symbol   of souls
finding themselves   lost and wingless

2. ISLANDED

O

yes. So true,
Your Majesty. Round as
we know God's world to be, O Queen,
without a doubt, Columbus fumbled. Isabella
gingerly taking in her hand his latest gift, the
black pimento grain brought from her new-found land
rolled one between thumb and finger, inhaled, then
imperiously crushed it, setting free all the spices
- Cinnamon Nutmeg Clove. It totally bowled
her over. Her Exchequer quickly took control.

Spices   worth   their   weight   in   gold

Worlds   to   be   crushed   for

their   spices   their   gold.

O

DISCOVERY

Always
          like the futile march of crab-armies
          from mangrove fortress to the beach
Always
          like the palm-fringe waiting
          to be breached

Already I know, the moment you land
I become islanded

In the shadows of the rain forest
I wait in submission

Amidst the trembling of the leaves
I practice hesitant discourse

Always
          my impenetrable heart.

THE BIRTH OF ISLANDS

Fire at the core
Necklace of ash, stone, coral.
Islands emerge, submerge or shift
with continental drift. Islands
are not immortal. Without you,
islands could never be. You
are the portal. Islands are born
from your longings.

See how easy:
        The spoon stirs up the void
        Seabird drops its egg
        A sand-grain launches itself

You blow breath on the ocean

Something breaks out on the face of the water

MESSAGE IN A BOTTLE

In its daily scouring of the rim of islands
the ocean prays for the invention of
postcards, telephones, E-mail,
transatlantic cables. Tired
of the tedium of reading
bottle mail and its futile blatherings:

> *Under a hostile sun I lie*
>
> . . .
>
> *From islands I want to be free*
>
> . . .
>
> *From savages, rescue me*
>
> . . .

Most times, the ocean can't be bothered
to deliver. Not even one decent poet
among them. The ocean itself can turn savage.

THIRTEEN WAYS OF LOOKING AT BLACKBIRD

(after Wallace Stevens)

I
The ship
        trips
into sight of land. Blackbird
is all eyes. Vows nothing but sunlight
will ever hold him now.

II
Survivor of the crossing, Blackbird
the lucky one in three, moves
his eyes and weary
limbs. Finds his wings clipped.
Palm trees gaze and swoon.

III
Swept like the leaves on autumn wind,
Blackbird is bought and sold and bought
again, whirled into waving fields
of sugar cane.

IV
Blackbird no longer knows
if he is man or woman or bird or simply is.
Or if among the sugar cane he is
sprouting.

V
Blackbird's voice has turned rusty.
The voice of the field mice
is thin and squeaky.
I do not know which to prefer.

VI
Blackbird traces in the shadow not cast
the indecipherable past.

VII
Blackbird finds thrilling
              the drum beats drilling
                            the feet of
men of women into
              utterance.

VIII
To Blackbird rhythm
              is inescapable
Fired to heights alchemical
the immortal bird consumed

Charlie Parker

wired.

IX
Blackbird once again
attempts flight. Crashes into
the circle's contracting edge.

X
Even the sight of the whip makes
Blackbird cry out sharply.
No euphony.

XI
Pierced by fear, Massa and all his generation
mistake Blackbird for the long shadow.

XII

Blackbird strips to reduce gravity's pull
readying for flight again. Fate hauls him in
to another impetus.

XIII

In the dark
        out of the sun
Blackbird sits
        among the shavings
from the cedar coffins.

MISREADING WALLACE STEVENS

'The birds are singing in the yellow patios'
Wallace Stevens, 'Like Decorations in a Nigger Cemetery' (1938)

On a day beloved of travel writers
the yellow of tropical, the pale green
palms upturned

the vivid birds preening
in patios overlooking a blue
denial

the world arranged just so
for the viewers.
Unseen

like decorations
in the cemetery right under
their noses

the graves
outlined in white bleached
coral, the conch shells

splayed like bones. Unseen
the mirror's solicitations
to keep the spirits

spellbound; the flowers faded
and torn, the crockery
decorations

broken and worn
like the folk
buried there.

In a moment of heightened interest
in something totally trivial
the visitors

are caught spellbound
by the sound
of a funeral

procession. A brass band.
And a choir of birds singing
in the yellow patois.

How exotic! the travel writers thrill.
How perfectly chic!
Understanding

not a word, they immediately
arrange for translation and
publication – each one

carrying home
a trophy recording and a wonderful
necklace of birds' feathers.

The funeral procession
passes into
the cemetery out of sight.

Unseen the black souls
now dressed
in white

singing in the yellow patois
accenting
towards light

REJECTED TEXT FOR A TOURIST BROCHURE

'I saw my land in the morning
and O but she was fair'
M.G. Smith, 'Jamaica' (1938)

1

Come see my land

Come see my land
before the particles of busy fires ascend;
before the rivers descend underground;
before coffee plantations
grind the mountains into dust; before
the coral dies; before the beaches
disappear

Come see my land
Come see my land
And know
That she was fair.

2

Up here, the mountains are still clear.
After three weeks, I heard a solitaire.
Down there, the mountains are clear-cut
marl pits. Truckers steal sand from beaches,
from riverbeds, to build another ganja palace,
another shopping centre, another hotel
(My shares in cement are soaring). The rivers, angry,
are sliding underground, leaving pure rockstone
and hungry belly.

3

No Problem, Mon. Come.
Will be one hell of a beach party.
No rain. No cover. No need to bring
your bathing suit, your umbrella.
Come walk with me in the latest stylee:
rockstone and dry gully. Come for the Final
Closing Down Sale. Take for a song
the Last Black Coral; the Last Green Turtle;
the Last Blue Swallow-tail (preserved behind glass).
Come walk the last mile to see the Last Manatee
the Last Coney, the Last Alligator, the Last Iguana Smile.

Oh, them gone already? No Problem, Mon.
Come. Look the film here.
Reggae soundtrack and all. Come see
my land. Come see my land and know, A-oh,
that she was fair.

MISSING

The last time I went home they told me you were missing.
For the first time since I'd known myself, you were not there.

For one so home-bound, who could have foreseen
such a dramatic ending: Missing Person. Presumed Dead.

Village fiddler, your playing was always out of tune.
Your choice of instrument that creaking violin: What

was it signalling? The ne'er-do-well? The one who failed
to make the grade? The only one who stayed?

Yet, your discordant life played out, I was amazed to find
you hadn't passed through like a false note a broken string.

You remained a vibrating source of conversation
an endless susurration. With the police indifferent,

your poverty-stricken neighbours hired a van
to take them on their own investigation across the river

to the rumoured scene of the crime, for they believed
you had been murdered. Theories were rife:

- *You know how he facety when he tek up his waters.*
- *He did get money so he boasy that day.*

Why had you taken that bus at all?
Where were you headed?

In a life devoid of excursions did you know
you were finally setting out to be tripped up by your fate?

Leaving home like that, you have missed so much:
Mass Dick's funeral, Tennie migrating, Pearlie and baby too,

Miss Carmen's husband dead. So many departed.
The young ones sit and wait. Not in the expectation

of any return. Waiting has become an occupation. A
permanent state. Abandonment the theme of this new life.

One day, I thought I heard you, Jumbieman,
unburied wandering spirit playing an unstrung fiddle

headed our way. Miss D who is the oldest person I know
said: *Nah, is you hearing bad. Ol' time sinting done weh*

Not even duppy bodder wid we now.
Yes, it's Version Time. Lyrics and licks. A life too raucous

for anyone to hear ghostly fiddlers again. Not you.
Not Tambu. Not Jonkannu. Not silenced Gumbay.

O Tambu you come back
but wha de use?
You come back but
wha de use?

HERE AND THERE

I knew I couldn't get there from here. Here
was the edge from which time slipped, objects

disappeared; the road slid from view,
voices sheared off as the paths veered. Here

was the dark, the damp, the steadfast dew,
the blue shadows following the sun as far as

here. Then stopping off to rest too long while
the lightness left, for there. Where was there, then?

Where the sky billowed. Beyond the curve of day.
So what alchemical light came through to point

the way, what magic words for the getaway?
For one day, I walked through without knowing

I had finally chewed into dust and absorbed
into my being the fibres of what it meant to be

Here.

Never knew that blue was a song to be sung,
no, never knew. Thought blue was something
swallowed: a choke, an anguish, an ache,
a separation from everyone, a curtain, an

emptiness, a disappearance. Thought I was
the only person who knew the meaning of blue.
I was very young then: pale, washed out, yet
already too far out to be extracted from indigo.

Thought blue was a lone sound, just one note
banged out on a piano key, in the tapping of
fingers to grate on the nerves, blue was for me,
solo. A game of solitaire, a disaffection.

Blue was like standing on that isthmus between
oceans, finding washed up on the beach
a lone shoe. Blue was not me and you, but me
or you. Avoidance the meaning of 'true blue'.

Blue was that in-betweenness, that moment
of change, of solstice, where you feared to fall
between worlds, into that blue crevice, become lost
in canyons and gullies, snow drift, millennium shift.

Blue was not that everyday gear that you wear:
blue jeans. No, blue was that covering for the
young dead, for the modest: the nuns, the
Virgin Mary, the untouched, the untouchable

life, the one you wanted to escape from, but
how could you? With the blue sky so unreachable,
the blue sea so unreadable, spattered only by flecks
of cloud, of foam like broken promises.

See now the blue smoke rising from morning fires
in the mountain cockpits, ephemeral sign
of the brother you'll set out to meet, to be greeted
instead by the smoke ring of the other: 'Me no sen,

yu no come.' You'll return to the blue-hollowed hills,
the shadowed evening, the slowing down of pulse
and heartbeat, to await the calling out by passers-by
of the saddest, the bluest, the most contradictory

words in the world: Good Night.

one day, strength (from
where, you don't know) to aim
for the opening, to say: I am leaving.
To walk to the edge of your feeling.
To load up with guilt (not a word
from the ones at the threshold). Not
a word! You keep walking. Down
the dirt track, to the lane, to
the street, to the highways of
the world. You alone. Not yet stunned
by the brightness. Not by hardness
of stone, of the pavement. No.
You say: I could get used
to the lightness.
                    Till the day
you're snared by another sensation:
on a hilltop, at that, you find yourself
drowning, a movement of ebbing
and flowing. You recognise early
(or too late) that you failed to detach
from that mooring.

Always, cruelty of choice.

Here's the knife.

Yourself:
            Executioner
Midwife

LOST TROPIC

Friend, I'm in a bad way, my skin
leaches out more tropic every day
like flood-prone mountain soil.

Left behind: uncompromised bones
like volcanic stones on hillsides.
Waiting. For Thunder.

Today, though, no rain. The Sky Shepherds
have corralled their flocks.

BLUE MAGIC CARPET

Driving up
        mountain trails
                to Cinchona

I'm not feeling
        the punishment
                of that dirt track

I'm not watching
        the curves
                nothing scares me

nothing
        not the precipice
                falling away

look way down
        not altitude
                look up there

nothing scares me in these mountains
        not even
                you leaving

to rock bottom I've fallen already
        see down there
                through undergrowth

dark as umbra
        look down

Then at the last bend
        as we enter the garden
                slowing down by the sinister Blue Gum

Look Up!
        The tone of your voice makes me look
            Can't stop

going Oh!
        I'd forgotten Agapanthus
            Hydrangea

famed blue hillside at Cinchona in May every year
        Now I'm touched
              Is that why you brought me

5000 feet plus
        up here?

Can't stop leaping out to fall on this carpet:
Agapanthus   Hydrangea. It's the acid that
does it turns it blue they all say. Can't stop
my own acid leaching away. To blue up
this carpet some more

Thinking   (for the first time in my life)
Thinking   I'm going to be alright
Thinking   The higher I climb the sweeter the air
Thinking the blues are getting lighter year by year.

MOON

I'm walking on this dark path overhung with hibiscus,
bougainvillea, when suddenly, an opening to the sky,
and in my face, this great, big, overpowering moon, in
silver. Thank you, Moon, for showing your most dazzling
self tonight, dimming the stars, seducing me from gloomy
thoughts, from citylight. I know it's your best face because
each month I watch you grow fat, then waste away on
some celestial diet before you disappear. No mystery
there. I know your ways. Soon a new you so svelte and
trim will start coming round again – until you lose control
and gorge to almost bursting. I can tell by your patina
on what you are feasting. This month it's the metallic you,
with hint of quicksilver, pewter, antimony. At other times,
there's the warmth of liquid amber, of honey. Though you
have never failed us yet, you tantalize with the uncertainty
of never knowing how big you'll get. That makes you
almost human. Not like that Sun who acts as if he's so
divine. I know comparisons are odious, dear Moon,
but such self-discipline is hard to stomach. He comes
showing the same predictable face day after day: no fat,
no shrinkage, no blemish. He does get a bit red and
wobbly some afternoons (bad-minded people say, from
drink!) .I'd like to think it's just that sometimes the old
fuddy-duddy can't wait till he's out of sight to change into
his old red flannel shirt and relax. By doing a two-step.

WILD NESTER

'Wild nester, wild nester so far from home
Wish I had the wings of a dove'
Traditional song

I   Wild Nester

By ones, by twos, the travellers return from winter faring,
their dress so elegant, their bearing like doctors
on their rounds checking me out to see
that all is not just well but as they left it. I feel them
soundlessly berate me with a look, criticize with a nod
between them: Why did she limb that tree? How goes
the Venerable Oak? How dare she suppress
Virginia Creeper's growth?

These birds I do not know as they do not know me; my
city backyard too confined for ceremonial introductions.
How I miss that vireo who shamelessly on arrival in the
south each June leaves everywhere amongst the leaves, its
vulgar and highly embellished calling card:

John Chew- it
John Chew- it
Sweet John Chew- it
Swe-et John   Swe-et John   Swe-et John

Faced with these northern scrutineers I ask myself: What
is the secret of making them yield their names, here in
a foreign land with no one over backyard fences to ask
anything. No Unka to whistle bird-calls. No Syl to tease.
No Jerry in the schoolyard to imitate the shy Mourning
Dove. No Bobby with his springe to capture Bald Pate.

No parrot in a cage to say even "Pretty Please".
No familiar Island Mockingbird to interweave with its
soaring imitative songs just a hint of its own troubles:

See me leg See me leg
Pain Pain Pain Pain Pain

None to give out a name.

II   Ping

                    Ya!

No Chicken Hawk to bait me while
next door my playmates sing

Bluebird Bluebird in and out the window
To see a rose again

Teasingly calling over the fence:

Buddy, Buddy come play with me
Put down your books and play with me

"No, I can't play I have to stay a yard
to keep Hawk from Auntie's Chickens."

Ping!

Primly. And pleased as puss that I'm
so important. They laugh. 'Chicken Merry
Hawk Deh Near' – like Auntie – I warn them

'Go weh' they cry and go back
to their playing. Soon my yard
feels too quiet

Ya!

Suddenly in the sunhot I shiver.
Auntie would say: Somebody's walking
on your grave, girl. Auntie knows
everything. But Auntie's not here.

  Ping Ya!

Auntie's far away. Shh! Mother Hen's
shushing her chickens. Shh!
The beat of wings?

      Ping Ya!

A shadow growing

       Ping Ya!
Chicks freezing
   playmates' voices
      across the fence

Put down your books and play with me

I try to answer

            Ping Ya!

But it's seizing

my voice

    my heart is

      its wings are

O Chicken Hawk
what will Auntie say? (I only
have time to think)

before

                      Ping!

        Ya!
Ping

III   *Blue Quit*

In Sweetwater Woods now
the Pea-doves are nesting

Across the blue water
my life is on hold

So what would I trade
to return to that place
to the blue hills, the hollows,
and bold Mistress Blue Quit
gossiping in the glade:

- *Sairey coat blue*
- *A true?*
- *True Blue!*

Hear her husband nuh, good for
nothing but nodding in the shade:

For true. For true. For true.

IV   White Belly

          and sometimes I'm that querulous
complaining White Belly Dove
and you its eternal interrogator:

- *Rain come wet me Sun come bun me O!*

- *Why don't you build a house?*

- *What's it to you?*

Yes,
What's it to you?

Sometimes I press my hands on the
top of my head to hold the lid on.
Tight. To keep the stories from spilling,

words from leaping into the glare of an
indifferent light. In Cockpit Country
deep caverns, dark secrets, blue endings
even now: *What Woodpecker say in him belly*
hard fe ansa.

For true. For true. For true.

V   *Blue Foot Traveller*

That world no longer exists.
Yet from the architecture of longing
you continue to construct a bountiful edifice.

This is not exile.
You can return any day to the place that you came from
though the place you left has shifted a heartbeat.

Like that artful dove Hopping Dick
you hopscotch.

3: PENNY REEL

I spy

a ribbon like a rainbow that loops out
and in like the dance round the Maypole
in the schoolyard. Girls to the left boys
to the right as weaving in and out we
make a basket. Skirts flashing, hair flying
for we've left it undone, turned it loose
– like the witches – to snare someone.

      Not knowing then, in the schoolyard by the sea
      that Death was that kindly old man
      who sat by the shore splitting reeds to weave
      his basket to capture fish

      that give the wrong answer

Little fishes in the schoolyard
skipping rope, looping rhymes:
                Little Sally Water
Hide and Seek
London Bridge is Falling Down
O the See-Saw
the Merry-Go-Round
swinging in the air, knowing
        the pendulum that swings always
                           stops.

    Then scurries back here.

With my little eye, what did I spy?

All passed through my mind then
like thread through the needle's eye
for nothing was I ready to see.

RIDDLE

Together, babe, we could have had the world sewn up.
You filled my eye, I kept you in stitches. When we
moved together we glided – no hitches. Yes, sometimes
I needled you. Too pushy, you claimed. But you – so
spineless, so easy, you always needed me to drag you
through. Yet, life's so unfair. For I'm the one left empty,
threadbare. While you, Mr. Sleazy, without me to keep you
on the straight and narrow, you still manage to thread your
way, tying everything – as you did me – up in knots.

The women of the family took tea all together except for
Aunt Millie, Uncle Vincent's wife. She read books, she

wore makeup and jewellery even on weekdays. On Sunday
afternoons behind locked door, she had me put colouring

(Madame Walker's, IMPORTED FROM AMERICA) in her
hair. She was a blue foot, a stranger, not a born-ya. She

had crossed water. They did not know precisely where
Uncle V had found her. He was the eldest, family head.

A sly dog and purse-string controller, so no one said
anything. Aunt Millie smiled often but her mouth was

sewn up. Her reticence offering them few strands,
the women of the family enhanced them with embroidery

(washing lightly in vinegar to keep the colours fast). From
her straight nose and swarthy skin they plucked skeins

to compose the features of a Jewess, or herring-bone in
the outside daughter of a rich merchant or plantation owner.

Her mother was someone mysterious, whipped onto the scene
with a slanting backstitch. She once sang opera?

She was said to be of Panamanian or Colombian origin.
Something exotic enough – like a french knot – to mistrust

but work in. They reviled Aunt Millie's use of scent. From
the few words they extracted they thought they detected

a foreign accent. Sometimes they feathered in 'Haitian',
infilled with dark threads to signify the occult powers

of that nation – how else could she have snared such as
Uncle V? They thought she kept her distance because

she was all of the above and snobbish. *My dears, such airs!*
She and I were *What a pair!* Myself, orphaned with frayed

edges unravelling into their care. Everyone knowing my
pathetic history, I could wind myself up in Aunt Millie's

mysterious air, undulate in the sweet waves (artificially
induced) of her hair. She nurtured me on books and

reticence. The women of the family fed me cold banana
porridge (or so everything then seemed) told me tales

of girls who did and men who didn't marry them. Tried to
enmesh me in their schemes to undo Aunt Millie's disguise.

In the end they embroidered her an elaborate cover when
(I could have said) a plain winding sheet would have suited her.

For to me she gave her story, unadorned. The women of
the family willed me their uniform tension. Aunt Millie left

me her pearls. I sold them, became a blue foot traveller.
Kept no diary. Sewed up my mouth. Shunned embroidery.

PENNY REEL

It is Saturday, the night of penny reel dances, girls in
pressed hair, white muslin and sashes, turn to
high-stepping gentlemen as they weave out and in
eye passing each other on the go-round.

The little dressmaker in the circle of light spilled from
Home Sweet Home lamp shade, sits sewing
at her straight-stitch treadle-foot machine, unwound
by the laughter, the fiddle and fife of penny reel.

Near the very same spot on the edge of the park where
the stark shanty-town edges in, there's
a Merry-go-Round. Her children she locks up inside
and away from temptation till she earns

enough pennies for their ride. She's not locked in.
It's life she's locked into. Can't remember
how she entered that ring. Can't see the revellers.
In a tenement room, there're no windows to outside:

every door in a row facing in. No wheel and spin.
The treadle-foot machine the go-round she rides.
But sometimes (she's noticed of late)
there's slippage, as with silk from her customers,

easy slide of her body to a pull from the outside.
Alone save the children, how unattached she feels.
Out there, her Saturday night sisters weave
something from life. Each reel a new set so the dance

might continue. Who decides on our measure?
She addresses this to no one in particular.
Her man could be anywhere: penny-reeling,
at his gambling, the bar. Perhaps (she is hopeful)

tonight he won't come. Forever. No more scars
on her body criss-crossing like ribbons. No more
riding her. No more grinding her down. No more
turning her into Ol'Higue. If she knew how to stop

having children she'd do it. But there's no one to ask.
Her sisters are all at the dance. Penny reel.
Thread reels her in. Three a.m. and she's
sewing for a Sunday delivery. Though the fabrics

are dancing, kaleidoscoping her eyes, her feet keep on
moving the treadle. Up and down. O Saturday night sisters
moving out and in to that rhythm of life.
But like her customers,

they too dissolve in her mind into parts custom fitted,
tape ribbon the only measure she knows.
And she? Do they see her as more
than a figure kneeling down to adjust the hems

of their garments, straight pins in her mouth. Do they know
she is coming unstitched? Sometimes
they don't pay her on time. Sometimes never.
And there's that Merry-go-Round. If she knew

how to rain curses down she would do it. But there's
no one to ask how to creep into houses, rip
their clothing to strips, tie as ribbons to the maypole,
and swing. If only she knew how to stop herself

wanting to fly through the walls as her feet work
the treadle. If only she could stay plaited up
like the ribbons round the pole. Stop reeling off
into this other. Not the straight-stitcher looking after

> the children but the one overlooking. The one
> who rips her skin, strips and discards it, so that
> bat-like, taking wing, she flies through the air,
> homing only to sound, to movement, the scent

of the dancers O my sisters who are reeling. She dives
for their blood. To suck up their being.
But the ribbons criss-crossed at the pole
are unyielding to witches or to humans

> who ribbon their skin. And because it is Saturday evening
> the one time in the week these lassies and lads
> are not grieving for homes left behind. Freed
> from labour, from tenement rooms, they abandon

themselves to each other. Keep dancing
till the dawn when witches must return to their skin.
Or be undone. Like the man coming in to curse her
– 'Ol' Higue' – when she asks where he's been.

> For its dawn. She needles him with her eyes.
> If she knew how to kill she'd do it but there's
> no one to ask. Her sisters still dancing. She finds herself
> knotting a thread round his neck. She jerks it. Bites.

There, it's done. But it's only one garment. Many more
till delivery. Sunday morning soon come.
Thank God for the dawning and the whisper
in the streets of the revellers passing, the girls

in crushed muslin, their hair now unpressed, the boys
still high-stepping. Easy passage tonight.
They have paid for the ride.
O penny reel dancers unreeling.

WHITE

'Take me and make me whiter than snow'
Protestant hymn

Nothing comes white here naturally, not unless
you count sea foam or cloud cap-in-hand begging
passage across the blue immensity. No snow-
scapes, sheep don't roam through here. Heaven
is where you have to go to become whiter than
snow. Or so they sing in the chapel. Try telling that

to Miss Dora the laundress who soaks clothes
overnight to let them know who is mistress then
beats them on the big rock and hangs them on
the bush to bleach in the dew. No speck permitted
to pass through her needle-eye scrutiny; the whites
she dips in a rinse of laundry blue to purge them

as sinners do with hyssop. Starch from cassava
grain Miss Dora uses to stiffen the clothes against
the playfulness of breeze that might see them
at their ease on the clothes-line and come tek fass
and undress them. Every weekday, Miss Dora's
laundry stays stiff and upstanding on the line,

like flags, in glorious array like cherubim and
seraphim, though Miss Dora don't business with that.
If you try to tell her that Heaven is the place to go
to climb the golden stair, turn sheep in the
shepherd's flock, become whiter than snow, she
will bridle and say, so what wrong with my big rock,

since when you dissatisfy with clothes scrub
on this washboard in tin tub, then how come you
never tell me you don't like how I starch, how I iron,
till now you have to go to some far away place
to obtain satisfaction? No, Miss Dora, you explain
(for Sunday being her rest day she has never

darkened church door), is skin we talking about.
If sin wash away in Heaven sinners come whiter
than snow. That's how it go. "Hm. Never seen",
she will say, "what they call snow or sheep. Some
speak of white foam on the sea but poor me never
been there yet. Plus if I was to leave the clothes

dirty, go walk bout, inspect the whole world, like
them bothersome young girls nowadays, what
those fine folk in the church would have to wear
come Sunday? Who to wash, starch and iron
the frills, who to stiffen the shirt collar, lay
the peplum straight, crease the pleat, who to make

even the worst sinner look neat and tidy as they
approaching what they call mercy seat, as they
walk up to this Heaven, fall in with the flock?
And another thing: Is this black skin I been living in
from I born. From morning, as you know,
the one thing I learn good is laundering. That

mercy seat, that heaven for me is the day I retire
from the work and put up my feet. So tell me
why I would suddenly want to be climbing up
golden stair, join some flock of sheep the first
time I setting eye on them. And when I get there,
why I would suddenly want my skin to turn white

as this shirt I just done wring out, start look like
that sheet on the line? If ever I should arrive at
them high-up place there, as a good washer
woman I couldn't hold mi tongue, I would
duty bound to say, "Lord, I glad I reach but I have
to beg you Sar, please go easy with the bleach."

LACEMAKER

(Valenciennes 1794)

Attached to my bobbins like the spider
I, with no time on my hands, spin out
a lifeline to hang on. Then I make
the noose: to form the hole I capture air
tangible as breath in this damp cellar. Round it,
I weave the thread in finest silk which will age
(unlike me) to palest cream, ecru, ivory,
age into 'charming old lace'.

I envy the spider her speed. In inches my life
edges by – (Her Ladyship so many yards for her ruff,
My Lord, years of work for each cuff, My Lord Bishop
three-quarters of my life to trim his alb).

Like the spider I grow brittle and dry,
like its web (pale and strong) my lace
(kept moist for good tension) surges on
fine as foam on the ocean which I'll never see.

For my eyesight's opalescent as shell now,
my vision translucent as pearl
yet my skeletons of thread stay delicate as webs
(like the fly, it's the holes I'm mesmerized by).

When I die, I'll go to my grave in coarse linen,
no edging. But my virginal hands will not cease
from signing *punto in aria*: stitches in air.
Never cease from making nooses for My Lord, My Lady.

Meantime, the spider and I wait
for our traps to be sprung

for lace-trimmed heads
to swing in bloodied air

(What a waste
of good lace

What a waste
of my lifetime).

PEARL DIVER

(Isla de Margarita, 1628)

Full fathom five
- or ten, my father
will dive from an open boat
each day. His body
is greedy for water.
Each night, he's caged
in a pen to keep him
chaste and dry as
the biscuits he's fed on.
No woman to stir him,
no water to wallow in;
were he to swallow a drop
next day he'd float like cork,
not go under. Be off our roster,
says Friar Antonio.
He'd never again
go down to the depths
to bring up Ave Maria
bring up sweet
Pater Noster.

Some days, no matter
how hard he plunges
my father surfaces
empty. Friar Antonio
calls it an insult
to Our Maker, caused
by thoughts of sin
(wet dreaming) and
has him whipped.

My father knows
the luck of the dive.
The only thing certain
is that till he dies, each day
he'll fall overboard
as the dew falls
into the open mouth
of the oyster.

BASKETMAKER

Already bestowed the accolades that mark you expert,
you still make baskets for the ordinary: the satchels,
the boxes, the quivers and fans that people need.
For each one marks a step on the journey to perfection,
the reeds in your hand a weave of your post-mortem fate,
each twist of your wrist a template of your soul's
patterning, your craft that will bear you up to the place
where the past masters dwell with the Divine Bird
of the Dawn.

Your hands cannot rest. After death you are still
compelled to weave as you navigate the final passage
where the dread Frog Mistress of Earth, arbiter of your fate,
scrutinizes every twist and turn. You could work
yourself up into such a state. But your entire life has led
you to this moment and as you weave your way your
course is set. Warp becomes worth. In twill and twist
of reeds you know you must entwine the divine, the
labyrinth unwind.

BIRD-MAN/ BIRD-WOMAN

'Over time, representations of the bird-shaman in pre-Colombian gold work evolved into heart-shaped icons.'
Gerardo Reichel-Dolmatoff, *Goldwork and Shamanism*

It takes heart to become one, the courage to be, to accept the separation from whatever life you embark from: the you who was never completed, the you who was never really there, the you now ripe for transformation into pure spirit of air. But first, in that extremity of solitude that is itself the first test, there is the you who have been chosen to endure the fortress of cold, the fiery furnace; the you who must fast to near-death; the you who must gorge on sacred tobacco juice day after day till the visions come easy; the you who must accept your terrifying gift of fore-seeing as the price of ecstasy; the you who at great risk must intuit and tame your guardian spirit; forge from bird song and calabash, feathers and spit, the implements of your sacred calling; the you who must practice hiring out your voice in the service of animals who will return it unrecognizably coarse but unsurpassed in its versatility; the you who must hang nine nights from the tree. At the end of all this suffering, you'll find the Spirit Death alone come to bear you away. But trust me. Purified, you will rise again another day as that other being, the one destined to serve, destined to cure, destined to recover lost souls, destined, Poet, to sing. But first, soul traveller, you have one more test to meet. Flight as the only way home. Come. The first lesson: how to fold your wings into a heartbeat.

ODE TO PABLO NERUDA

1

You did say:
Don't call up my person
  I am absent.

But your signs are still decipherable in the pure stone,
in water, in the palm-prints of the labourer. And by those
who like me seek the pure voice untrammelled, the courage
to speak of things nobler than the self, to write impure
poetry that bears witness to the raw and the natural, to be *the*
voice from the bottom of the well.

I want to pay homage but here in the north,
separated by a continent from Santiago, Isla Negra,
or my own island home, so far from the sea I can't strike
the right chord; the measure that I tread moves no one else.
I find myself drifting and wordless.

So I turn to find again something you said
about grasping poetry like thread?
Here it is:

You must spin it
fly a thread
and climb it . . .

This isn't a matter
for deliberation
it's an order.

Neruda's words are in italics

But away from the elements of which my life has been spun
I can't even remember what the knot stands for
that I'm feeling in the thread that fills my hand now.
The thread tying up the bundle of How-It-Was. The thread
that I cling to though you've said poetry is of the here-and-
now *revived by the light of each new day.*

The here-and-now eludes me and I worry about clinging
too tightly to this thread. For what happens if it becomes
too knotted to decipher, too clotted with blood, with mud
from the traveller, too broken to tie again, too ravelled,
too threadbare?

What if you use it all up – for a clothesline that breaks,
for a leash the dog runs off with? What if there's no thread
left? And no more where it came from? There, I've said it.
What if you confidently go to bed leaving a spindle of new
thoughts to be processed. Next morning you reach for the
thread and it's gone like smoke – it's cobweb you're left with.

So Pablo Neruda, although I absolutely agree with many
things you have said this thing with the thread I find a bit
slippery as if you'd reeled it off without thinking and simply
disappeared leaving in the blue this monstrous kite

and me
the one
holding
the string.

2

This thread of poetry: Where does it come from?
Are you born with it? Is it handed to you like a sweet
or a rattle to a child, who takes it without thinking?
As I took your kite string?

Here's how I see it: This thread is one that crosses your path
like the spider's web. You walk through unaware
The Great Spider still clings to it. So now Spider clings
to you, my friend. This is not an accident. You have been
chosen Spider's apprentice. To master language. As
Trickster, to spin and weave tales. To prophesy and heal.
The go-between serving earth and sky. Sometimes the
messenger left dangling.

After you have taken the thread – the thread you cannot refuse
– you must choose how to handle it. You might cut off bits
to skip rope with or play cat's cradle. That's fine for joy
needs to unwind. But there comes a time when you might be
forced to confess: I don't know what I did with the rest of it.

For one day – it's like that scenario that tantalizes in our
nightmares, only this one is real – one day, you are caught
in a dragnet. After your arrest you are brought to account
before some tribunal that will throw the book at you charging
you with theft.

Of what? You will ask. And Neruda will reply: For not
repaying your debt of poetry to the people who forged you
your good life with their blood and their sweat.
All you had to do was weave the thread
into cloth
for those who have

only rags,
nets
for fishermen . . .
and a flag
for each and every one.

You may plead Not Guilty. But perhaps you have already
been weighed and found wanting:
There are some poets so big
they don't fit in doorways
and some merchants so sharp
they don't remember being poor.

If found unconvincing you'll be disconnected, cast away.
Alone, you're left knotted up and wordless.

3
Here's the real trick (and no one ever tells you this):
The thread of poetry to safely travel, the knot of yourself
you must first unravel.

You have to bathe in your own grave
and from the enclosing earth
take a look upward at your pride. . . .
Then, you learn to measure
You learn to speak, You learn to be.

Stripped
and skeletal
you first
navigate
the crawl-space
that allows you

to enter
the labyrinth

blindly
you must
trace every inch
of the root's meander
the convolutions
of the vine
the veined stem

you must take the measure
of the thread born from root
reed stem or fleshy leaf

the thread purged of sap or resin
retted
scourged and riven
to expose its gut.

Immersed
in water
to cast off
impurities

its fibrous heart
elucidated

its old skin shed

you'll
encounter

the thread

born again

as sinews of rope
its tensile strength
corded

The thread that can now
be woven
into strong linen

Like jute fibre
meshed into string

Or like reeds, criss-crossed
into sound centered
at the cross-roads
where the crack
of the whip now
deflects evil forces
clears a path.

If you find yourself
back here
You have mastered
the first trick.

You
can make your way
through the needle's eye
pulled up
by the thread
of your poem

dragged down
by the weight
of words
waiting
to be strung.

The real apprenticeship
has begun.

4
So this knot that I've been feeling, this pearl of anxiety
I'll make part of this rosary of the Alpha and Omega
which could serve as the necklace for Brahma
for Buddha Muhammed the Virgin Mary for Oya.

But really it need not be more than my simple mnemonic
to remind of that journey I myself took long ago through the
roots through the vines. The songs of the heartwood,
the calligraphy of the veins of the leaves
almost lost in my meanderings.

I needed, Neruda, this kite-string to jerk me back to the
source of creation, to that mantra of obligation

A chain-link of miles strung out across oceans
a creole spider-work of many hands.

The beads telling not decades but centuries.

Like this strand of those ancestors handed a one-way
passage to the clearing-house for the convict, the criminal
and cut-throat, the patriot and the rebel,
the pious pilgrim, the debtor, the poor, the downtrodden,

the foolish, the brave heart, the no-hope younger son.
A lifeline to the plantations – the only one other than
swinging as seaman, as buccaneer, as pirate from the rigging,
the yard-arm, the gallows.

Here's a bead
for the spirit necklace
of that other lineage.
The ones bound in chains
dragged across the Atlantic
in vessels, full-rigged.
Their vocal chords ripped
with their names
on the tips of their tongues.
Washed away in salt water
the cartography of home.

Survivors of these crossings transplanted shoots, planted
their children's navel cords to become
the roots and the vines for my string.

And a special bead
for a few I never knew:
the ones who flew
the ones who didn't touch salt
so stayed fluid as air
light as the web of the spider.
Flew back on the wings
that they wove from obligation
pulled by the strings
of ancestral desire.

But the ones that will never die out are too gelatinous
to be strung, being seaweed themselves like floating

sargassos on the currents of life. Spirit pirates with no roots
of their own. The same ones who forged the chains of
indenture, brokered sugar cane sweetened with slave blood.
Their tentacles still as far-reaching and fatal as the
entanglements of the constrictor of vegetal growth: the
Strangler Fig.

So much more unstated as my legacy. Not found in my
blood but possessing me. The fibres of belonging to this world.

5
I've had to weave a cloth to wrap it all up in, a bundle for
carrying for I'm travelling too. But not flying – too much salt
in my veins.

I've been seeking a thread to tie up the bundle which has been
growing unwieldy with the cries and the whispers of the ones
I can't name: The lost ones, the limboed, the un-cared for,
the un-loved. The mortified, the discarded, the "disappeared".
All resting uneasy on my conscience. Along with the poems
I failed to deliver or neglected to write and not
saying: "I love you" enough.

Yes, we each have our measure, and our burden to carry
but sometimes the cries are so piercing, we are silenced.

And
there
are
times
like this
when
having

crossed
the abyss
I want
to feel
free
to fly
kites
if I wish
or just
dangle
from
a thread
like
the
spider.

So I'm seeking that old woman, the wizard of the cords
who used to tie up the wind with three knots in a bundle
and sell it to sailors: "Mark well, my good man. Loosen
this knot for light breezes, this one to send you clipping
along and this – woe betide – for a battering."

Yes, I let loose the hurricane. And I'm sorry about the
damage but I forgot which knot was which – that's the
problem with raw thread it – all looks the same. But my
hurricane heart feels better for its roaring, for scouring
the world. For it's the strong wind that cleanses, that
unburdens and purifies. It uplifted the fallen. And broke
the thread. But I'll mend it and restring with fresh beads.

6

I wanted more than woman's knotted portion so I refused
to learn the way of thread: sewing, embroidery, darning,
weaving, tapestry, knitting or crochet do not appear on my
CV.

But look at this:

In the sky
a kite
still aloft
and the one
holding
the thread
is me.

Maybe I'll accept after all my commission as apprentice
Spider who spins from her gut the threads for flying,
for tying up words that spilled, hanging out tales long
unspoken, reeling in songs, casting off dances.
And perhaps for binding up wounds?

With strips and remnants left over (and with bits and pieces
of this kite I'm reeling in) I can make a costume for the
dancing fools the masqueraders who dress in rags and tatters

Egungun
Jonkonnu
Pitchy-Patchy
Pierrot and Gombay

the ones who dance the ancestors.

Perhaps when they dance they'll let the wind spin their strips
and their tatters into thread flying ready to be climbed.

Or feather them into birds on the ascendant, their wings
lightly stirring up the ocean below the Middle Passage.

Perhaps they'll spin off into rainbow-hued streamers
plummeting the spaces of Earth into which all those
millions 'disappeared'

Awaking and setting free the dreamers.

For sometimes

It's hard to tell
if we close our eyes or if night
opens in us other starred eyes,
if it burrows into the wall of our dream
till some door opens.

7

And so, my trickster powers evolving, I'm learning like you,
Pablo Neruda veteran tightrope walker, to swing more easily
between joy and obligation.

Here it is: this poem I've made for you like a quilt from thread
and strips as a way of thanking you – not for all your other gifts
(for that would require a book) – but simply
in exchange for your kite which – as you have seen – I've
turned to good use.

And for allowing me to explore boundlessness.

For witnessing how the thread of poetry can serve for
binding up and for un-binding. And for the bounty of these
lines which have unwound themselves

8
"God is dead" wrote Nietzsche.
"Heaven is empty"
wrote Kandinsky,
"God is dead".

You, Pablo Neruda,
saw instead

The heavens
unfastened
and open.

GARDENING IN THE TROPICS (1994)

G
O
G O U R D
R
D

hollowed dried calabash
humble took-took how simple
you look. But what lies beneath that crusty
exterior? Such stories they tell! They say O packy,
in your youth (before history), as cosmic container,
you ordered divination, ritual sounds, incantations,
you were tomb, you were womb, you were heavenly home,
the birthplace of life here on earth. Yet broken (they say)
you caused the first Flood. Indiscretion could release from inside
you again the scorpion of darkness that once covered the world.
The cosmic snake (it is said) strains to hold you together for what
chaos would ensue if heaven and earth parted! They say there are
those who've been taught certain secrets: how to harness the power
of your magical enclosure by the ordering of sound – a gift from orehu
the spirit of water who brought the first calabash and the stones for
the ritual, who taught how to fashion the heavenly rattle, the sacred
Mbaraká, that can summon the spirits and resound cross the abyss
– like the houngan's asson or the shaman's maraka. Yet hollowed
dried calabash, humble took-took, we've walked far from that
water, from those mystical shores. If all we can manage is
to rattle our stones, our beads or our bones in your
dried-out container, in shak-shak or maracca, will
our voices be heard? If we dance to your
rhythm, knock-knock on your skin,
will we hear from within, no
matter how faintly
your wholeness
resound?

hollowed
dried
calabash
humble
took-took
how simple
you look

TRAVELLERS' TALES

MEDITATION ON YELLOW

'The yellow of the Caribbean seen from Jamaica at three in the afternoon.'
Gabriel García Márquez

1

At three in the afternoon
you landed here at El Dorado
(for heat engenders gold and
fires the brain)
Had I known I would have
brewed you up some yellow fever-grass
and arsenic

but we were peaceful then
child-like in the yellow dawn of our innocence

so in exchange for a string of islands
and two continents

you gave us a string of beads
and some hawk's bells

which was fine by me personally
for I have never wanted to possess things
I prefer copper anyway
the smell pleases our lord Yucahuna
our mother Attabeira
it's just that copper and gold hammered into guanín
worn in the solar pendants favoured by our holy men
fooled you into thinking we possessed the real thing
(you were not the last to be fooled by our
patina)

As for silver
I find that metal a bit cold
The contents of our mines
I would have let you take for one small mirror
to catch and hold the sun

I like to feel alive
to the possibilities
of yellow

lightning striking

perhaps as you sip tea
at three in the afternoon
a bit incontinent
despite your vast holdings
(though I was gratified to note
that despite the difference in our skins
our piss was exactly the same shade of yellow)

I wished for you
a sudden enlightenment that
we were not the Indies
nor Cathay
no Yellow Peril here
though after you came
plenty of bananas
oranges
sugar cane
You gave us these for our
maize
pineapples
guavas
– in that respect
there was fair exchange

But it was gold
on your mind
gold the light
in your eyes
gold the crown
of the Queen of Spain
(who had a daughter)
gold the prize
of your life
the crowning glory
the gateway to heaven
the golden altar
(which I saw in Seville
five hundred years after)

Though I couldn't help noticing
(this filled me with dread):

silver was your armour
silver the cross of your Lord
silver the steel in your countenance
silver the glint of your sword
silver the bullet I bite

Golden the macca
the weeds
which mark our passing
the only survivors
on yellow-streaked soil

We were The Good Indians
The Red Indians
The Dead Indians

We were not golden
We were a shade too brown.

2

At some hotel
overlooking the sea
you can take tea
at three in the afternoon
served by me
skin burnt black as toast
(for which management apologizes)

but I've been travelling long
cross the sea in the sun-hot
I've been slaving in the cane rows
for your sugar
I've been ripening coffee beans
for your morning break
I've been dallying on the docks
loading your bananas
I've been toiling in orange groves
for your marmalade
I've been peeling ginger
for your relish
I've been chopping cocoa pods
for your chocolate bars
I've been mining aluminium
for your foil

And just when I thought
I could rest
pour my own

– something soothing
like fever-grass and lemon –
cut my ten
in the kitchen
take five

a new set of people
arrive
to lie bare-assed in the sun
wanting gold on their bodies
cane-rows in their hair
with beads – even bells

So I serving them
coffee
tea
cock-soup
rum
Red Stripe Beer
sensimilla
I cane-rowing their hair
with my beads

But still they want more
want it strong
want it long
want it black
want it green
want it dread

Though I not quarrelsome
I have to say: look
I tired now

I give you the gold
I give you the land
I give you the breeze
I give you the beaches
I give you the yellow sand
I give you the golden crystals

And I reach to the stage where
(though I not impolite)
I have to say: lump it
or leave it
I can't give anymore

For one day before I die
from five hundred years of servitude
I due to move
from kitchen to front verandah
overlooking the Caribbean Sea
drinking real tea
with honey and lemon
eating bread (lightly toasted, well buttered)
with Seville orange marmalade

I want to feel mellow
in that three o'clock yellow

I want to feel
though you own
the silver tea service
the communion plate
you don't own
the tropics anymore

I want to feel
you cannot take away

the sun dropping by every day
for a chat

I want to feel
you cannot stop
Yellow Macca bursting through
the soil reminding us
of what's buried there

You cannot stop
those street gals
those streggehs
Allamanda
Cassia
Poui
Golden Shower
flaunting themselves everywhere

I want to feel:

you cannot tear my song
from my throat

you cannot erase the memory
of my story

you cannot catch
my rhythm
(for you have to born
with that)

you cannot comprehend
the magic

of anacondas changing into rivers
like the Amazon
boas dancing in my garden
arcing into rainbows
(and I haven't had a drop
to drink – yet)

You cannot reverse
Bob Marley wailing

Making me feel
so mellow

in that Caribbean yellow
at three o'clock

any day now.

HURRICANE STORY, 1903

1

Time and time again, Grandmother plucked
bits of fowl coop from the pinguin fence.
Grandfather drained his fields, shored up
their lives against improvidence.
When the earth baked hard again, into
the forest he walked to cut the thatch
to patch his house. Corn drying in the husk
he hung from the rafters while afu yam
and sweet potato ripened (safe from
breeze-blow) underground.

2

When the wind rose in '03, he opened his
tin trunk, took his good clothes out
and packed the corn in. Granny topped it
with cassava bammies and chaklata balls
with a nutmeg and cinnamon leaf tied
with string. After the storm, Granny
would extract milk from fallen coconuts,
make coconut oil to fry the bammies, grate
corn to make porridge, melt the chocolate
in hot milk with cinnamon and nutmeg
to give us courage.

3

In those days storm warning came by
telegraph to Postmistress. Living in
the bush, Grandfather couldn't see her
rush to broadcast the news by posting
a black flag. But he was the seventh son
of a seventh son and could read signs
and interpret wonders so when the swallows
flew below the roof line, when the sky
took on a special peach glow, when flocks
of birds sailed west over the hill,
when clouds banked at the far side and the air
was still, he knew it was time to batten down.
Into the house Granny brought her goat
and fowls – though in the excitement,
two birds fled.

4

Grandfather knew just when to board
the last window up and brace the door.
Noah's Ark was never as crowded and wet.
Thatch blew about and whipped our faces,
water seeped in, but on Grandfather's bed
we rode above it, everything holding
together. For my grandfather had learnt
from his father and his father before him
all the ways of orchestrating disaster.
And my grandmother schooled on Sankeys
led us in singing. In our frail bark
in total darkness we passed through the eye
and out the other side, till all was still.

When Grandfather opened the window the sun
was shining.

Granny hitched up her skirt and petticoats
to unseemly heights (we children had never
seen so much skin). Stood waist deep
in the water in her yard and searched
the blue skies for a sign as Noah's wife did.
She found it when her missing sensay fowl
and favourite leghorn rooster turned up safe
but ruffled, having spent the night together
in the hole in the Cotton Tree.

And as we put our lives back together
I too young to be schooled yet on disaster
spent my time watching that sensay fowl that
strutting leghorn rooster, dying to be
the first to see the strange bird fated
to be born out of that great storm.

MOONSHINE DOLLY

Each full moon

I lay flat on the ground
with outstretched limbs
while you outlined my body
with bits of glass, mirrors
stones.

I would rise
leaving Moonshine Dolly
my ghostly self
behind.

One night
flat on my back
gazing at the full moon's face
I was too scared to rise
for *she* was pulling and pulling –

"Get up," you said,
"You're spoiling the game."

To Moonshine Dolly I whispered: "Hold me tight."

For she was pulling so
and if I rose
you'd run to grab hold
and you'd rise too

and all the children
would come running after
and there we'd be
holding on to each other

leaving far below

Moonshine Dolly
gazing
at this chain of children
rising and rising

to the moon.

HURRICANE STORY, 1944

Each weekday morning
my father the dandy put on
his bicycle clips
his straw boater
and pens lined up in pocket
hair slicked down
vowels well oiled
he rode off to work at
Solomon's Drygoods and Haberdashery
where he was assistant (white-collar class)

Every Sunday
dressed the same way to flaunt his glory
he pedalled uphill for miles
to where his navel-string was buried
and when he left
freewheeling downhill
his barefoot country brothers
ran long distances behind
falling back from exhaustion
while their pride
their hope
kept riding
on that frail back

Then (his mother complained)
before he get establish and
help his own family to gain
their due reward
as is only right and proper
as it ordain (as it set out in the Good Book amen)

he take up with this girl
that don't come from nowhere
she dark she plain
nobody know what
he see in her when
a man his calibre could get
any girl he want (little most)
Mark My Words
she going cause him to turn down
again

But through her
they got the house
for though he was a gentleman in good employment
(first class) it plain to see
(she of few words said)
one body money can't stretch

She turned back to the soil

You see what I mean his mother said
also: you mek yu own bed you must lie on it
and: we all have we own row to hoe

My mother who hardly ever spoke
crooned hymns in the garden
to her skellion tomatis pumpkin melon
which thrived (as everybody knows)
from her constant labouring
(nothing like a pregnant woman to encourage
pumpkin and melon)
she sang mournful hymns as she reaped
sang as she took her crops to market

My father never wanted
a higgler for a wife
never wanted to turn back
to that life he'd escaped from
never wanted (in public)
to acknowledge this rooting
to the soil

But the house must be paid for
(though nothing for insurance)
the children fed
sent to school

In '44 when the hurricane struck
it all came unstuck
the roof the fields the job
(for Mr Solomon lost his shop
and laughingly retired on *his* insurance)

My mother clapped her hands and
ordered us children
to comb the nearby fields
for battered planks
and twisted corrugated zinc
ordered us to climb up
nail the roof back down
ordered us to thank the Lord each night
for what we were about to receive
– black cerassie tea and water crackers –
ordered us early in the morning
to come into the garden before school
to pick caterpillars
off tomatis and melon
ordered us to grow straight
like skellion

My father stopped putting brilliantine
on his hair
his vowels went flat
as the tyres on the bicycle he finally sold
to buy us schoolbooks
he never noticed we had stolen his pens (telltale ink
leaking from our pockets) never noticed
the battered straw boater disappear
(jauntily reappearing on top of our mother's
head-tie as she strode off to market one day)

No job he could find
worthy of a man of his abilities
(his mother agreed)
couldn't turn back to the muck
when his hands had been clean for so long
something bound to turn up

Meantime
he coasted downhill
and we settled into our new routine:
Monday Tuesday Wednesday our mother worked in the fields
Thursday Friday she went to market
Saturday she left him money on the dresser
He took it and went to Unity Bar and Grocery got drunk
came home and beat her
Sunday she went to church and sang

CAT'S CRADLE

Playing
cat's cradle

I could tie
the sun up tight

there'd be no night

but then with endless day
you'd stay out there so far away
playing out your lines

and I'd be here
playing cat's cradle.

Without you

too long
the day

I untie
the sun

You haul in
the night.

CARIBBEAN BASIN INITIATIVE

'The canoes being small… the water lapped over the edge in an
alarming way. Had any of us sneezed… we must have foundered.'
Mary Kingsley, *Travels in West Africa*, 1897

1

Like limpets we cling
on craft that ply
in these waters
where our dreams lie.

Afraid to draw breath
lest we stir up
the waves, our faces
might crack but no smile
will spill out; a look
can cause listing: we all
look within; we know
to keep still, we are
still in our graves.

2

No sailor am I.
I was farming
till my seed
failed to yield
fell on stony
ground. I cried:

What is harder
than stone?

Never knew
at the time
the answer is:

Water.

3

My mother sought a sign
in the basin.

She said: sky's so clear
nothing's given back here.

I said: Agué Lord of the Sea
rules over me.

You can't keep
a good man down,

if you born to hang
you can't drown.

4

So many passengers
we listed; so much
bailing out as we
drifted, our numbers
kept shrinking and as

the nights passed,
our bodies got lighter
so we were never sinking
as low as some
we never saw rise again
out of that water.

Not all trunks will float.

5

Marceline and Anselm
unseasoned young men
went into the forest
to cut the tree for
their boat. It's funny
how grudgingly that
tree fell. Funny how
each day it grew back
again. They never could
hollow it enough to
make it float.

Never send a boy to
do a man's job, I say.
They will not follow
the old way.

Feed the spirits before
you feed the children.
Before you make the first
cut, you must pay.

Some rules cannot
be flouted. Some gods

will not uphold
the unconverted.

Agué Lord of the Sea:
Watch over me.

6

After weeks of
dead reckoning
no beckoning
landfall; I hang
by a thread
to my dream.
We were seeking
the Gulf Stream:
it is we who
are found.

Reclaimed,

we are bound
for an island
a stone's throw
from our own.

No mariners here.
Here there be
Marines.

Yes, Sir!

7

What is stronger
than stone?

Nothing's stronger
than this cage
on Guantánamo,
nothing's bounded
as this rage
as this basin.

Yes.

Sir!

8

louvri baryè pou mwen

9

They're shipping me home.
I've been spared
to navigate again
some other dry season.

Though we drift
past all sign
past all meaning
past all reason

Though we see
in the basin
white sand
from our bones

Though we thirst
till we die
surrounded
by water

Like limpets we'll cling
on craft that ply
in these waters
where our dreams lie.

HURRICANE STORY, 1951

Margaret and her man Delbert
such a fine young couple
everybody said
so full of ambition
so striving
their little boy so bright
so handsome
so thriving

Though in 1951 after the hurricane
struck they ended up suck-
ing salt same as everybody else

Margaret said: look
we'll never get anything back together
unless we do something serious
something really ambitious
Plenty people going to England now
plenty women going in for nursing
Let me go
while you continue here
with the farming
Just for the
time being
As soon as I
graduate I'll come back
get big job
That time see me in
mi whites nuh
Soon turn Matron

Together
we can build a good life
for our son

But somehow she never
got far with the nursing
for in her life she never
knew people could hard so
never thought a country could cold so
With her heart turning into stone
with nothing to show for it
- she wanted so much
for the boy – she decided
though she would continue striving
she wouldn't write again
until she could send him
what amounted to
something

The man begging his mother
to keep the boy said: so-so
farming can't take us too far
This can never provide my son
with the life I want for him

He set off for America
to be a farm worker
Every year he went
to pick oranges

Those on his tree
in his yard
turned black from blight
for he never came back
to that piece of ground

He settled in the city
Got married
Sometimes (when prodded)
he sent something
for the boy
He had
other things
on his mind now
He was ambitious
and striving again
Going far

Granny said
to the boy:

Hard-ears children
can't reach nowhere
you will
never amount
to anything

His ears
weren't hard
he was just
hard of hearing
After a while
he also
stopped speaking

His granny wrote
to his father (whom
he couldn't remember)
to come and get him
saying:

I old
I can't strive with him
any more

His father saying
he would try with him
came and took him home and
introduced him:

This is your sister Rose
This is your brother Reuben
This is your sister Carol Ann
This is your brother Jonathan
and this is your new mother
Miss Sharon (a lady who looked
as if she had learnt to smile
out of a book)

After a while
they said he was too hard-ears
to amount to anything
and left him alone

He'd go by the shore
and practise writing
(without a pen):

First he blew breath
across the water
"Ah-"

After that
every day
he'd go and call out
Ah
O
Ah-o
Ah-o
Ah –

He threw the sounds across
the ocean like stones hoping
they'd hit
something

rebound off

someone
he couldn't give
a name to

but only by an echo
returning
would he know:
the ocean wasn't as empty
as he was

Every day now

Ah-o
Ah-o
Ah

Till one day
he managed:

Ah-o
Ah-o
Ma-

Soon the sounds
would make syllables
the syllables
would make words
the words
would make phrases
the phrases
would make poems

His mother
would never read them
she was too busy
swabbing out
a hospital
in Reading
England

After so many years
she no longer even
thought of him
(or anything else
for that matter)
gazing

day after day
into
that
pail
of water

Until
one day
as she sluiced out
a ward
she fancied she heard
someone
calling her name

Ma-

It sounded as if
it came
from the
pail
it sounded like
her rightful name
(not the name
– Miss Black –
by which she
was known here)
No one here
knew *that* name

Ah-o
Ah-o
Ma –

Each day
she poured
more and more
water
on the floor
to try and
capture
that sound

Miss Black
Matron said
(finally)
this just
won't do

No she said
turning the taps
on full
flooding
the ward
pouring out
an ocean
from her pail

Standing
by that shore
she clearly heard
her name now

Ma –

I must go she said
taking off her shoes

I must go now
taking off her overalls

I must go to my –
stripping off her clothes

– son

in Aenon Town, Jamaica –

stepping into
the water
(as they rushed
to restrain her)

– my son
my s –

.

Standing on that far shore
he heard at last rebound
the sound he'd sent
though slightly bent
by distance

and without conscious intent
he started walking

to meet it

ILLEGAL IMMIGRANT

If I never make this uncharted
         passage
one way or another, never tell
         my children
their insolvent eyes set me
         sailing.
To reach, no ocean's too wide
         for the leap
no depths too deep to be
         plumbed
no body too shiftless to fit
         this dugout.

STOWAWAY

There's this much space between me and
                              discovery
a hairline fracture getting wider with
                              each wave.
I feel it, though I cannot see to
                  hold
my thoughts together – they're
                              running loose
all over; someone's bound
                        to trip,
I know it. One day light will enter
                        this grave.
Till then, I let my thoughts go.
                        Dangerously
unstrung, I dive deeper into this
                        fault, this
undeclared passage. Without soundings
                        there's no telling
how unfathomable the fall, how
                        attainable
the littoral. Surfacing
                        I'll dangle
on a single hope: that my eyes
                        be blinded
only by the promised land.

MEDITATION ON RED

'I feel I've been here for... centuries. Even this winter dates
from the dark ages.'
Jean Rhys, letter from Cheriton Fitzpaine, Devon

1

You, voyager
in the dark
landlocked
at Land Boat Bungalows no. 6
never saw this
green
wide
as the sea
green
limitless
as the rain
that greeted your arrival
at Cheriton Fitzpaine.

You (destiny:
storm-tossed)
never saw
the rolling downs
patchworked
in emerald, peridot
mint, celadon
never saw
sheep
tossed here and there
like foam
for decoration
on this green

quilt
of Devon.

Arrival
at Land Boat Bungalows
at flood time
never rid you of
the fear of being
the fear of being left
the fear of being left
  high and dry

so at no. 6
there was
perpetual flooding
so much drink
flowing
so much tears
so much
on the edge of
but never quite
under
that quilted
green
comforter
wishing for
blue skies
wanting
but never quite
believing
your craft
to be
worthy.

Such
disappointing
harbour
(again).

"It is very cold," you write
"It gets dark early.
One meets dark figures…
frost and ice are everywhere."

You still had
this burning
desire
to set sail
even though
(now and always)
and despite
what long ago
the fortune teller
said –
"I see something great
in your hand, something noble" –
you were
rudderless.

Marooned
in the grey
you decided
to garden.

Since
they called you
witch
you would

conjure up
bright
flowers
spelling
each other
all year.

In spring
(you wrote)
you planted seeds
"I wanted heaps of poppies

Not one came up."

Instead
(you wrote)
there was sometimes
"blue murder
in my wicked heart"

and a red dress
in your closet
a "Christmas cracker dress"
– the whole village knew and whispered
waiting for another explosion

(like that
which long ago
came
from the
attic).

But you
in your housecoat

frayed
round the edges
like you
red
like your rages
(soothed
with a box
of pills, red
what else?)
found
there were
occasional
red-letter days:
a dream of red
and gilt
a dream of
getting your face
lifted
buying
a bright red wig
to shock
and a purple dress
with pearls
to hoist
your spirits
(when you voyaged
out).

Meantime each day
you made up
your old face
carefully
for the village
children

making faces
at you
who knew
how to spell

little knowing
in that grey mist
hanging over
Cheriton Fitzpaine
how cunningly
you masked
your pain
how carefully
you honed
your craft
how tightly
you held
your pen
how brilliantly
you planned
to write
(though they
no doubt
heard it
as "ride")
across that
Wide Sargasso.

2

Now in the time
of that incredible green
again

in spring
in rain
I come
to the churchyard
at Cheriton Fitzpaine
Devon

knowing
you're there
Lady
sleeping it off
under that dark
grey
stone
though it says
in a categorical
tone:

HERE LIE BURIED THE ASHES
   OF MY BELOVED MOTHER
JEAN RHYS, C.B.E., NOVELIST
   (ELLA GWENDOLEN HAMER)
         BORN
DOMINICA AUGUST 24TH 1890
         DIED
   EXETER MAY 14TH 1979

   "GOOD MORNING MIDNIGHT."

I've come to
wake you
with spring flowers
(the ones
you had no
luck with

growing)
– snowdrops
daffodils
narcissus

knowing
you would prefer
a blanket
of red
– flame of the forest
hibiscus
heliconia
poinsettia
firecracker
bougainvillea –

for of
Mr Rochester's
first wife
you said:

"she is cold
– and fire
is the only warmth
she knows
in England."

I apologize.

Right now
I'm as divided
as you were
by that sea.

But I'll
be able to
find my way
home again

for that craft
you launched
is so seaworthy
tighter
than you'd ever been

dark voyagers
like me
can feel free
to sail.

That fire
you lit
our beacon
to safe harbour
in the islands.

I'd like to take
with me
a picture

and though
you were never one
for photographs
or symmetry
(except
in fiction)
it's to be taken
by the woman
who typed

your last
book.

And though
I know you hate
to be disturbed
just
when you've finally
settled
down
I beg you
to tear yourself
away
from that grey stone
in the churchyard
at Cheriton Fitzpaine
for just one moment
and –

Look,
Miss Rhys:

No rain!

- and see
Mary Stephenson
standing there
at her ease
waiting
to say
to us both:

"Smile please."

HURRICANE STORY, 1988

My mother wasn't christened
Imelda but she stashed a cache
of shoes beneath the bed.

She used to travel to Haiti,
Panama, Curaçao, Miami,
wherever there was bargain

to catch – even shoes that
didn't have match. Back home
she could always find customer

come bend-down to look and talk
where she plant herself on
sidewalk. When the hurricane

hit, she ban her belly and bawl,
for five flights a day to Miami
grounded. No sale and her shoes

getting junjo from the damp (since
the roof decamp) and the rest
sitting in Customs, impounded.

My mother banked between her
breasts, lived out her dreams
in a spliff or two each night.

Since the storm, things so tight
her breasts shrivel, the notes
shrinking. Every night she there

thinking. Every morning she get up
and she wail: Lawd! Life so soak-up
and no bail out. To raatid!

I was beating chaklata when someone
came shouting: A stranger man come!

I dropped everything. Same way
in my sampata, my house dress,

my everyday head-tie, I rushed to
the square wondering: could it be?

How many gathered there so long
after our men disappeared into

the black water dividing us from
Puerto Limón, Havana, Colón

knew it was he? Not his sons lost
to a father fifteen years gone.

There he was. Leather-booted and
spurred, sitting high on a fine horse.

Never spoke a word. This Spanish
grandee sat on his horse and

looked at us. Looked through us.
Never could lump poverty. Used

to say: Esmie, when I strike it rich
in foreign what a fine gentleman

I'll be. And you with your clear
complexion will sit beside me,

your hands stilled from work
like silk again (silk of my skin

my only dowry!) Ashamed now of my
darkened complexion, my work-blackened

hands, my greying hair, a loosening
of my pride (three sons with Mr Hall

the carpenter who took me in) I
lowered my eyes and tried to hide.

I needn't have bothered. He looked
so troubled, as if he'd lost his way.

And suddenly, with nothing said,
he wheeled his horse and fled.

And ever after we talked of the
wonder of it. The stranger never

spoke to anyone. Forgotten the young
man who left home with a good white

shirt (stitched by these hands) and
a borrowed black serge suit (which

the owner never recovered), a heng-pon-me
with four days ration of roasted salt fish,

johnny cakes, dokunu and cerassie for tea
to tide him over to the SS *Atrato*

lying in wait in Kingston Harbour.
All, all the men went with our dreams,

our hopes, our prayers. And he
with a guinea from Mass Dolphy

the schoolteacher who said that boy
had so much ambition he was bound

to go far. And he had. Gathering
to himself worlds of experience

which allowed him to ride over us
with a clear conscience. I never

told anyone. For I would have had
to tell his children why he hadn't

sent money for bread, why his fine
leather boots, why his saddle,

his grey mare, his three-piece suit,
his bowler hat, his diamond tie-pin,

his fine manicured hands, his barbered
hair, his supercilious air. Never

was a more finely-cut gentleman
seen in our square. And I trembled

in anger and shame for the black limbo
into which my life had fallen

all these years till my hands touched
the coarse heads of my young sons

recalling me to a snug house clad
with love. And I cried then, because

till he came back I had not known
my life was rooted. Years later,

I learned that his fine gentlemanly air,
his polished boots, manners and Ecuador

gold bought him a very young girl of very
good family in Kingston. And they wed.

He, with a clear conscience.
She, with a clear complexion.

NATURE STUDIES

PLANTS

Plants are deceptive. You see them there
looking as if once rooted they know
their places; not like animals, like us
always running around, leaving traces.

Yet from the way they breed (excuse me!)
and twine, from their exhibitionist
and rather prolific nature, we must infer
a sinister not to say imperialistic

grand design. Perhaps you've regarded
as beneath your notice, armies of mangrove
on the march, roots in the air, clinging
tendrils anchoring themselves everywhere?

The world is full of shoots bent on conquest,
invasive seedlings seeking wide open spaces,
matériel gathered for explosive dispersal
in capsules and seed cases.

Maybe you haven't quite taken in the
colonizing ambitions of hitchhiking
burrs on your sweater, surf-riding nuts
bobbing on ocean, parachuting seeds and other

airborne traffic dropping in. And what
about those special agents called flowers?
Dressed, perfumed and made-up for romancing
insects, bats, birds, bees, even you –

– don't deny it, my dear, I've seen you
sniff and exclaim. Believe me, Innocent,
that sweet fruit, that berry, is nothing
more than ovary, the instrument to seduce

you into scattering plant progeny. Part of
a vast cosmic programme that once set
in motion cannot be undone though we
become plant food and earth wind down.

They'll outlast us, they were always there
one step ahead of us: plants gone to seed,
generating the original profligate,
extravagant, reckless, improvident, weed.

STARAPPLE

Expect no windfall here.
Don't stand and wait
     at this portal between
shadow and light.
Two-sided starapple leaf
     can't be trusted as guide.
Without force, starapple
     won't let go of its fruit.
Too afraid you'll discover
     the star already fallen
     the apple compromised.

PINEAPPLE

With *yayama*
fruit of the Antilles,
we welcomed you
to our shores,
not knowing in
your language
"house warming"
meant "to take
possession of"
and "host"
could so easily
turn hostage.

Oblivious
of irony,
you now claim
our symbol
of hospitality
as your own,
never suspecting
the retribution
incarnate
in that sweet
flesh.

So you
plant pineapples
arrayed in fields
like battalions
not knowing
each headdress

of spikes
is slanted
to harness
the sun's
explosions

and store them
within
the fruit's
thick skin
on which
– unless
you can peel
them off quick –
pineal eyes
watch and
wait,
counting
down.

MADAM FATE

When
Lucifer
fell
he landed
on our pasture.
He rose again
posing
as innocent
star-flower.
Penetrating
his new guise
we recognize
notorious
Madam Fate,
her poison
as potent
as his
last
drop.

FERN

1

Fern inherent
in this spore
uncoils
the green leaf
into light
on branch's
brown
recoil.

2

Fern was present
at Creation fired
the carbon of
revolution fuelled
the age of industry
in which inheres
its diminution.

MOUNTAIN PRIDE

Like Mountain Pride
every September
I go hurtling off cliffs
      hurtling off cliffs

again.

SUN AND MOON

Moon's
desire
to play
with
fire

caused
Sun
to run.

Let's
pray
they
stay
that
way.

SNAIL

O snail
so slow
so low
we can hardly
stoop
far enough
to see
outlined
behind
what might be
the cosmic
trail.

GUAVA

Than guava fruit
nothing sweeter
so free in its wild simplicity
so generous
it makes itself available to all comers
– even the worms.

GUAVA/2
(for Myrth)

Maud was making guava jelly
when she said to me: "I don't
like it when guava tree starts
to bear too much. I take it
as a sign. Remember that time
in Barbados?"

… that house scented with guava
and Maud trying to reduce the vast
quantity of fruit you kept harvesting.
That week she made guava jelly, guava
cheese, guava paste, stewed guava,
and blended the pulp into drink.
But your tree would not stop
producing. It bore faster than she
could cook or we could consume.

I think of you, stricken so suddenly.
I say nothing. To her it would seem
extreme if I said that the Taíno
zemi of the dead is called Maquetaurie
Guayaba – Lord of the Guava – and that
it is he who instructs the tree when
to speed up production so that
the incoming soul will have enough of
the fragrance of guava to feed on.

GUINEP

Our mothers have a thing
about guinep:

Mind you don't eat guinep in your good clothes.
It will stain them.

Mind you don't climb guinep tree.
You will fall.

Mind you don't swallow guinep seed.
It will grow inside you.

Our mothers have a thing
about guinep: they're
secretly consuming it.

No one today regards anatto and guinep
as anything special.

No one puts them on stamps or
chooses them

for praise-songs or any kind
of festival.

Country people one time used anatto
to colour their food,

these days you can hardly get it
not even at the market.

As for guinep: that's worse. Big people
scorn it

(though they eat it). Only children confess
they love it.

Well, with the Taíno and others who were
here before us

it wasn't so. Nothing could happen without
anatto paste

or guinep stain to paint their bodies
with.

Guinep black to summon the rain clouds;
anatto red

for war. They also used both for things
in between like

medicine and curing or birth or death.
Patterns in red

or black were to them like dressing up
for occasions.

They wore these colours on their bodies
as we wear clothes:

to protect themselves, to signify or
engage in play,

as markers on the road of life or as
flags signalling

in the most straightforward way:
Look at me:

I'm beautiful! So give a thought to
forgotten anatto

to humble guinep and the memory
of the ol'people

who weren't the first to wear them
anyway:

How do you think Moon got stained
black like that?

What do you think Sun used to redden
its face?

PAWPAW

Everybody likes pawpaw
but some don't like it planted
too near the house.

Me too.

I know for a fact
that tree will sap your strength
waste your muscle
draw you down
to skin and bone.
To nutten.
An ol'lady
told me that.

It's better to plant it
the far side of the fence.

You can laugh
and call it superstitious
nonsense
but if you want proof
just wrap pawpaw leaf
round a tough piece of beef
or mutton
and wait
and see
if it don't draw it down
to nutten.

Just like the ol'lady did say.

BAMBOO (*IN FIVE VARIATIONS*)

1

"Bamboo love" burns
bright and hot
and comes (and goes)
in flashes

Leaving behind
as residue
fugitive
bamboo ashes.

2

Bamboo prides itself on knowing
the art of living long:

Before wind, rain, axe and forager
humbly bending

while secretly sending deep into
cliff or mire

roots that are grasping and strong,
to spread. Not always

as quickly as that dread enemy
of conceit: fire.

3

If Stone had been a better debater,
Man (like Stone) would be living
forever. But long ago when such
matters were settled, Stone lost
the argument for eternity to Bamboo.
The clincher came with Bamboo saying:
it's true, this way Man will die,
like me. But look along this endless
river bank, what do you see? So Man
could be. With careful tending,
despite my periodic ending, from
my roots young shoots spring, routinely.

4

Cows grazing on fresh bamboo shoot
gaze at eleven-year-old me lying at
bamboo root, in my sanctuary: dried bamboo
leaves my bed, my head buried in a book.

"The Little Prodigy", my Great-Aunt
Emily (sarcastically) calls me when
I refuse to help her dust or cook,
polish silver or learn to use a hook

to fish up thread or wool in her tortures
called crochet and knitting. To keep her
from having further fit in my idle
presence, at my earliest convenience

I take off over the picket fence, across
the pasture to lie in that dense bamboo
thicket. All who pass by call out to
remind me that Duppies inhabit bamboo root

and if I don't take care those spirits
will cause my head to twist around, my
tongue to tie, my eyes to shoot up
straight out of my head as bamboos do

from the ground. Still, as often as
possible I perversely choose to lie and
court fright on dry leaves that rustle,
under bamboo joints that creak, troubled

only by the thought that Great-Aunt Emily
would experience such delight if a Duppy
(or the cat) actually got my tongue.
"A nice kind of heathen we're raising"

she says talking over my head to some
invisible presence Up There (for such
weighty matters to me cannot be
directly communicated). And only because

I said Church Makes Me Sneeze (which is
true). In view of her great age and to
avoid further outrage I bite my tongue
and wisely don't say that if she would only

leave me alone, one day in bamboo cathedral
I might encounter even the Holy Spirit,
for there I find I can breathe in (without
sneezing) a naturally fresh and liberating air.

5

You say you've been to my house
in the hills and never heard
from my high window

something like a dry rustle
from the river-bank, a long blue
sighing? Yes, maybe (as you say)

it wasn't the wind dying
in bamboo leaves and yes maybe
that isn't the sound of wild

bamboo flutes scaling up and down
mountain passes which I keep
hearing from this high window

near St Clair Avenue Toronto
Canada which is not where
river-bank or hill is.

GARDENING IN THE TROPICS

Gardening in the Tropics, you never know
what you'll turn up. Quite often, bones.
In some places they say when volcanoes
erupt, they spew out dense and monumental
as stones the skulls of *desaparecidos* –
the disappeared ones. Mine is only
a kitchen garden so I unearth just
occasional skeletons. The latest
was of a young man from the country who
lost his way and crossed the invisible
boundary into rival political territory.
I buried him again so he can carry on
growing. Our cemeteries are thriving too.
The newest addition was the drug baron
wiped out in territorial competition
who had this stunning funeral
complete with twenty-one gun salute
and attended by everyone, especially
the young girls famed for the vivacity
of their dress, their short skirts and
even briefer lives.

Gardening in the Tropics we revel in
Hot Tropical Colours. My father's land
was blue. In his prime, his banana
plantation came right to our doorstep.
We lived deep in this forest of leaves
made blue by the treatment against
Leaf Spot Disease which he humped around
the fields in a battered spray-pan. On
Banana Day (which I think was Wednesday)
we went off to school eyeing all the way
the bunches wrapped in blue banana-trash
waiting at the roadside for the truck.
We fervently prayed ours would find
acceptance in the sight of the Inspector
for every bunch was earmarked to pay for
something. Sometimes it was shoes. We
didn't choose those in Hot Tropical Colours
since each child could have only one pair
(for school and chapel) and we were taught
only black or white would find favour
in His sight

                                         But all this was ages ago.
             We children fled the blue for northern light
                 where we buy up all the shoes in sight.
                    My closet is filled – finally – with a
              rainbow of shoes in Hot Tropical Colours
            (which look marvellous against the snow).
               My father's house (I'm told) is visible
             from all directions now (some crops grow
          only in young gardens). Alone, fanning sand

and stoning breeze, my father lets in all that air,
let's that Hot Tropical Sun pour down
to fill his blue lungs and warm
his old and vegetating
bones.

FINDING YOUR STONE

Gardening in the Tropics
you never know what you'll
turn up. Yesterday it was bones,
today: stones. Here's one
that might be holy. To test,
tie white cotton thread
around it. Hold over a flame.
If the thread doesn't burn
you've found it: a power stone.
Breathe lightly on it to confirm.
You see it sweating? Even the gods
perspire. Take your *pierre* home
and feed it. The heart gets weak
if the spirit is kept
too dry.

THE KNOT GARDEN

Gardening in the Tropics,
you'll find things that don't
belong together often intertwine
all mixed up in this amazing fecundity.
We grow as convoluted as the vine.
Or wis. And just as quickly!
Only last week as our leader left
for another IMF meeting, he ordered
the hacking out of paths and
ditches, the cutting of swaths
to separate out flowers
from weeds, woods from trees. But
somebody (as usual) didn't get it
right (what goes on in mixed
farming is actually quite hard
to envision since so many things
propagate underground, by
division). Returning, our leader
finds instead of neat trench
and barricade separating species,
higglers and drug barons moving
into the more salubrious climes
while daughters of gentry are
crossing lines to sleep with
ghetto boys with gold teeth
and pockets full of dollars
derived from songs on the hit
parade. In the old days, he'd
have ordered some hits himself
but agencies that give aid
are talking human rights now.

Instead, something more subtle
– like poisoned flour or raging
tenement fires – is allowed
to spread. While citizens are
dying our leader is flying again,
off to another IMF meeting
in the presidential jet high
above this dense tropical jungle.
Meanwhile, the fertilized soil
(nothing like fire to do it)
bursts into new and twisted growth
of such profusion by the time
he returns, it proves
too impenetrable for landing.
Avoiding confusion, our leader
travels on, searching for
unencumbered skies, over the
Cayman Islands, or Liechtenstein,
or Geneva.

THE COLOURS OF BIRDS

Gardening in the Tropics, part of the ambience
derives from the presence of Rare Tropical Birds.

I like it when the parakeets come calling; they
never fail to amuse and entertain. Did you know

it was because of their antics that the Great
Anaconda Monster was finally slain? They made him

laugh – and in so doing expose his tongue – which
the hummingbird (according to plan) pulled out

by the root; the other birds then set to and
killed him for in his skin, his blood, his viscera

and his tongue, the monster had kept for himself
all the colours of the sun. Till that deed was done,

all birds were colourless. After the killing, they
dipped their bodies, legs, heads and beaks into the

palette of Anaconda's remains to stain themselves with.
Some are such show-offs now, you'd never believe

they came from such tame stock – those families like
the Macaws, the Hummingbirds, the Parrots and others

I could name and that in any case in the colour
domain the spirit of the Anaconda – as the Rainbow –

continues to reign pre-eminent. But to get back
to the deed. The silly little parakeets just kept on

dancing, making faces and laughing fit to kill so that
by the time they came to their senses it was done

and the other birds had taken their fill, daubing
themselves with every tint under the sun except that

vibrant green which the (now) brilliant wits said was
startling, yes, but too incredibly jejune if made

a whole suit of. To their yellows, blues and reds
they touched just a smidgen so quite a bit was left back

(which is a good thing for parakeets travel in enormous
packs) and they had to be content with that. They

were not (so they tell) they were so irritated
they squabbled and yelled and threw paint and daubed

at one another till each got deeply saturated with this
vivacious green colour – the exact shade of young

maize (which is why to this day parakeets attack
fields of it since they assume those stationary

birds are mimicking them). In the evenings when
they're flying home I hear them noisily complaining,

still blaming each other for their (almost)
monochromatic lot. Which is why the old ones (for

moral edification and with malicious intent) love
to tell a story about humans: the tale of the

would-be beauty queen who sits in the asylum forever
trying to wash off her skin the stain from those

tropical impurities showing through, that made her
a darker hue than the winner. Poor thing (the

malicious gossips sing) she still hasn't learnt
that throughout our tropical domain, people may all

look different but, unlike the birds, so proud of
their assorted strain and their varicoloured plumage,

that other monster has not yet been slain. So when it
comes to the colour of skin, pigmentation is not yet in.

THE TREE OF LIFE

Gardening in the Tropics was easiest
before the Flood. We had just one tree
to care for – the firstborn, the Tree
of Life. When (after the Great Fire)
the earth was bare and we were starving,
The Mighty One took pity and planted
deep in the interior a tree so
ubiquitous it bore on its branches
food of every different kind. Mapuri
the wild pig discovered it but kept it
hidden, sneaking off behind our backs
to eat his fill. But we suspected
something so we sent our most
skilled detectives to make him spill it.
First, Woodpecker, but he couldn't help
stopping to tap at every charred stump
– which alerted Mapuri to our plan;
others tried, but it was Rat
who succeeded. Of course, Rat being
rat, he tried to keep it hidden too,
but crumbs on his whiskers betrayed him.
We had to threaten to kill him before he
took us there. In front of this
unimaginable tree we fell down and
praised Him – and then we ate our fill.
After that, we merely had to reach
overhead to pluck a nice juicy starapple,
then perhaps a naseberry or two
before gathering for cooking fresh ears
of corn, hot peppers and tomatoes
for seasoning, cassava to make bread

and drink for celebrating.
So imagine our dismay when out of
the blue His voice came one day and said:
Cut the Tree Down! We trembled, but obeyed,
chopping away for generations
until it swayed and fell (water already
starting to trickle from the hole left
by its root – but that is the start of
another tale). He ordered us to take from
the branches slips and cuttings and plant
them everywhere. And that is how we
acquired crops for cultivating. From
that time, I've been a convert of
mixed farming though, of late, I've
noticed the agricultural officers
(those long-sleeved white shirt boys)
have been coming around to try and
persuade us to chop everything down
and plant only one crop. They say we can
get more money that way – from exporting.
But it's only the young ones they fool.
It's true they're all driving fancy cars
now, they have tractors, big houses,
are sending children to school. But let
them wait till drought or blight
comes round. What will they eat?
You see me here? I'm sticking to the plan
of having all my food, my seasonings and
medicines mixed up in one ground. For if
He wanted us to plant just one thing
in the garden, why did He make us chop
The Tree of Life down?

SEEING THE LIGHT

1

Gardening in the Tropics nowadays means
letting in light: they've brought in machines
that can lay waste hundreds of hectares
in one day, they've brought in (since we have
already passed this way) other peoples to hack
and burn through; smoke obscures the sun for
months now, there are not enough trees to pull down
the rain. The animals are gone too; without hunters
they're no longer game. By the time they've cut
the last tree in the jungle only our bones
will remain as testament to this effort to bring
light (though in their chronicles they might have
recorded it by another name: *Conquista?*
Evangelismo? Civilizacion?)

2

Before you came, it was dark in our garden,
that's true. We cleared just enough for our huts
and our pathways, opened a pinpoint in the canopy
to let the sun through. We made the tiniest scratch
on Mother Earth (begging her pardon). When we moved
on, the jungle easily closed over that scar again.
We never took more than we needed. Always gave back
(to Earth) our thanks and our praises, never failed
to salute the gods of the rain, the wind, the sun
and the moon in her phases. Never failed to provide
tobacco smoke for the spirits to feed on that show us
the game. When the yuca or the maize was ripe,

we celebrated. By the stars and planets across
the green (and dark) terrain, we navigated.
In all of this, we took up so little space,
it would have been easy for you to greet us
when you came – and move on. There was enough
in the jungle to provide gardens for everyone.
All over these green and tropical lands there
could have been pinpricks of light filtering
through the leaves to mirror the stars of Heaven,
invert the Pleiades.

3

But from the start, Earth did not please. You
set it alight, you disemboweled it, you forcefully
established marks of your presence all over it.
As you tore up what sustained us, our world
under your sway fell into the true darkness
of Night, fell apart from lack of regulation.
For we no longer had power to summon the spirits
with tobacco, with invocations to harness the
blessings of the sun, the rain. You told us your
one God had the power to bring us the true light,
but we've waited in vain. To this day – as catastrophe
holds sway and earth continues to burn – there are
things we still cannot learn. Why did those
who speak of Light wear black, your colour
of mourning? Why was their countenance so grave?
Why on a dead tree did they nail the bringer
of light, one Cristo, torture and kill him
then ask us to come, bow down and worship him?
Yet, with all the strange things that have happened
to us since your first coming, it's not so hard perhaps

to believe that in some far-off land this Cristo,
this person who had never heard of us, was
nevertheless put to death, gave up his life,
in order to enlighten us. Maybe many more trees
must die to illuminate his death, as many leaves
must fall to cover up our dying.

AMAZON WOMEN

Gardening in the Tropics, sometimes
you come across these strong Amazon
women striding across our lands –
like Toeyza who founded the Wori-
shiana nation of female warriors
in the mountains of Parima – of whom
the missionary Brett and Sir Walter
Raleigh wrote. Though nobody believed
them, I myself could tell a tale or two
(though nothing as exotic as the story
of Toeyza and her lover Walyarima who
swam the river disguised as a black
jaguar whenever he visited her). Now
we've got that out of the way let me
hasten to say I'm not into sensationalism,
I merely wished to set the record
straight by averring that the story
of Amazon women might have begun
because when the warriors went away
– to war or voyages – it was the
women who kept the gardens going
and sometimes if the men were not
heard from again (as occasionally
happened) they banded together and
took up arms to defend the territory.
So somebody – like Cristobal Colón
or Sir Walter Raleigh – could have
come along and heard these (marvellous)
tales of (fabulous) lands full of
(pure) gold and fierce (untamed,
exotic) women (you know how men stay!)

And the rest (as they say) is history.
Mark you, the part about Toeyza's
husband sending her and the other
women to gather cassava for a feast
while he ambushed and killed her lover
is true (at least, my auntie says so
and her husband's uncle's grandfather
told him as a fact – and he got it
from someone who knew). I don't know
about you but the part I find
disgusting is that while they were
away, the husband (a chief at that)
skinned and hung the lover up
in the women's hut as a lesson
to faithless wives. (Though if men
go around in jaguar disguise, what
can they expect?) If you ask me,
that husband got what was coming
(poisoned with bitter cassava juice
mixed in with the beer) though
I can't see what the rest of the men
did to deserve equal treatment.
But that Toyeza (with liberated words)
led all the wives in flight and they
managed (despite pursuit) to fight
their way across the jungle to the
heights and freedom in their own
nation which ever since has been
justly celebrated as the Land of
the Amazon. The best part (I hear)
is that they allow men to visit them
once a year. Boy children they send
back to the land of their fathers,
girls they keep to rear (though

I'm not sure I would want my girl
raised by a band of women outlaws
keeping company with jaguars). But
you see my trial! I'm here gossiping
about things I never meant to air
for nobody could say I'm into
scandal. I wanted to tell of noble women
like Nanny the Maroon queen mother
or the fair Anacaona, Taíno
chieftainess who was brutally
slain by the colonists, or of
the Carib women whom the said Colón
relied on for navigation
through the islands. I hadn't meant
to tell tall tale or repeat exotic
story for that's not my style.
But we all have to make a living
and there's no gain in telling stories
about ordinary men and women.
Then again, when gardening
in the Tropics, every time you lift
your eyes from the ground
you see sights that strain your
credulity – like those strong
Amazon women striding daily across
our lands carrying bundles of wood
on their heads and babies strapped
to their breasts and calabashes of
water in both hands.

TROPIC LOVE

Gardening in the Tropics you hear poetry
in some unexpected places. Sitting on my
verandah last night I overheard two people
passing by. The woman said:

> You don't bring me flowers anymore
> – or anything for the children.
> My heart has turned to stone
> but I cannot put that in the pot.
> Love me and my family or leave me
> to sit by the roadside to sell,
> by the riverside taking in washing,
> by milady's fire cooking for my living.
> I'm a woman with heavy responsibilities.
> With my lot I'm prepared to be contented.
> With your sweet words, Lover, tempt me
> not, if you've come empty-handed.

THE IMMOVABLE TENANT

Gardening in the Tropics, sometimes
you come across the most unreasonable
people. Like some tenants (who are

in exactly the same position as me,
it's just that some of us don't
quibble; we accept our lot and cope).

Next door, there's this lady, old as
Methuselah. You'd think she'd yearn
for peace and quiet now since

in her lifetime she's experienced
nothing but upheaval and a succession
of husbands, each one claiming

to be lord of the manor, each
fading from the scene leaving her
as lonesome queen or bereft first lady.

That's because, although they all
liked to pretend they were of enormous
net worth, having title to prove it,

everyone in this area is mortgaged
to the limit to landlords up north
– or bankers across the sea.

And, as my old daddy used to say,
he who pays the piper calls the tune,
or, he who wields the big stick

gives the lick. In my neighbour's
case it's a former husband's uncle
who's as cantankerous as they come

– and rich as Croesus – and as dumb.
Well, perhaps not quite, for he
managed to acquire all that property.

Now he has to go out of his way
to defend it, feeling it gives him
a right to interfere in the business

of all his neighbours to ensure
that none falls sway to other
foreigners and sells out for nothing

(as the old lady's husbands did
– to him). It's no joke, for once
or twice when a few of us in the area

started talking to potential investors
about new types of development for
our holdings, the man turned nasty,

introduced strong-arm tactics, and
worse, threatened to cut off our access.
That's serious, for while we were

composing calypsos, dancing sambas
and generally fooling around, he was
out there buying up not just all our

ground, but the very air we breathe;
he's rented our air spaces, taken
control of our seas and beaches;

underground he's taken mining leases
and overhead he's set up satellite dishes.
We all live in dread that we can't

mash ants without his knowing. On top
of it all, he's acquired rights (from
God knows where) to dump (if he wishes)

his garbage on our shores. You see me
here? I'm not lying: when I was younger,
I joined in some protests, gave him

a little scare, I'm not boasting but
maybe a bomb or two had my signature on it,
as did petitions. But that was before

I came to hold him dear. If you play
ball, he'll treat you fair, throw things
your way, include you in the game.

I tell my people now to cool it. For
I've been paid to see the wisdom of
supping with the enemy especially if he

has the longest spoon, the biggest stick,
the deepest pocket. Seeing as how
we're such good buddies now, he's

asked me as a favour to talk to my
neighbour for she's messing up his plans
for that property. He's spent a lot

of money fixing up the place, he wants
to attract tourists, investors and
extractors, for the garden is full of

trees ripe for felling and the house
of treasure priced for selling and there
are minerals to be mined. Everything

is on time, all the necessaries (with
my help) have been dealt with, the right
palms greased, contracts signed.

It's just this miserable old lady living
(on borrowed time) in the basement now
– though he's fixed it up fine. She's

constantly undermining him, screaming
at his tenants and everyone within
hearing (even over his airwaves): "Beware!"

Then she wraps her head in red, puts on
her mourning garments and stalks the
streets disguised as the dread Warner

Woman calling out "Fire! Blood! Repent!"
It's making the tourists and investors
jittery and since it might cause them

to move to a more inviting continent,
she's spoiling it for all of us here,
for people up north (except for Uncle)

can't distinguish one place from an-
other in this hemisphere. What annoys me
is, that old woman is not as mad

as she pretends. My advice would be
to evict her forcibly (precedents
having been set with her husbands

and other malcontents). I'm sure
most of the neighbours would assist
for Uncle has been generous with arms

for self-defence. Though a few
(down the road on the left-hand side)
can be counted on to encourage her

rebellious pride, in the final analysis,
we shall overcome, for we have might
– and right – on our side. It's just that

something about the old woman (which
I can't put my finger on) disturbs me.
When last I met with her, I left her

ranting (as usual) about Uncle tearing
down the old places and rebuilding with
(she says) unseasoned lumber and other

inferior material. She cites this as
another example of environmental
betrayal (for despite her age, she's up

on whatever topic is the rage). She
claims that her father after cutting
timber, waited centuries for it to render

all that stored up water before using it
for building. That way, the occupants
might have come and gone but

the structure lived on. She says these
hurry-come-up schemers build on sand.
She's watching them fill up their pockets

but she knows once the going gets rough,
the digging too tough, they'll leave,
abandon her house and land, jettison

their efforts to the jungle. As soon as
they spy next door the fabulous new
virgin territory – they'll move on.

To add to my discomfiture, each time
I'm leaving, that crazy lady croons:
Strangers might occupy my house and land

from time to time. But from this redoubt,
I always repossess it, inch by inch.
With the help of the steadfast tropical

sun, wind and rain, with the help of the
termites, the ants, the wood lice and
the worms, I always reclaim. I can wait,

unforgiving. Unlike the rest of you
who slaughter time, I've learnt the art
of eking out my living.

GARDENING ON THE RUN

1

Gardening in the Tropics for us
meant a plot hatched quickly,
hidden deep in forest or jungle,
run to ground behind palisade or
palenque, found in cockpit, in
quilombo or *cumbe*. In Hispaniola,
where they first brought me
in 1502 in Ovando's fleet,
as soon as we landed, I absconded
and took to the forest. Alone,
I fell in with runaways who
didn't look like me though
(I took this as a sign) their
bodies were stained black (with
grey markings) – in mourning
they said, for the loss of their
homeland, else they would have
been painted red. The bakras
called them wild Indians, me they
called runaway, maroon, cimarron.
No matter what they called, I
never answered. As fast as they
established plantations and brought
millions like me across the sea,
in chains, to these lands, the
dread of mutilation, starvation,
transportation, or whip, counted
less than the fear of life
under duress in the Americas.
The brave ones abandoned plantation

for hinterland, including women
with children and others waiting
to be born right there in the
forest (many mixed with Indian),
born to know nothing but warfare
and gardening on the run. With
the children, no opportunity
to teach lessons was ever lost;
nothing deflected them from
witnessing:

*Copena, charged with and convicted
of marronage... is sentenced to
having his arms, legs, thighs, and
back broken on a scaffold to be erected
in the Place du Port. He shall then
be placed on a wheel, face toward
the sky, to finish his days, and
his corpse shall be exposed. Claire.
convicted of the crime of marronage
and of complicity with maroon Negroes,
shall be hanged till dead at the gallows
in the Place du Port. Her two young
children Paul and Pascal, belonging
to M. Coutard, and other children
– Francois and Batilde, Martin and
Baptiste – all accused of marronage,
are condemned to witness the torture
of Copena and Claire.*

2

Some have said that, compared
to many, when my time came, I
got off lightly. The first time
they recaptured me they cut off
my ears and branded me with a
fleur de lys on my right shoulder.
I ran away again. The second time,
they branded me on the left side
and hamstrung me. I crawled back
to the forest. The third time,
they put me to death. Released
from all my fears now I feel free
to enter their dreams and to say:
You might kill me but you'll never
bury me. Forever I'll walk all
over the pages of your history.
Interleaved with the stories
of your gallant soldiers –
marching up the mountainside
in their coats of red, running
back (what's left of them) with
their powder wet, their pride
in tatters, their fifes and drums
muted, their comrades brutally
slain by the revolting savages
(who cowardly used guerrilla
tactics, sorcery, stones for shot
and wooden replicas for rifles)
– you will be forced at least
to record the presence of their
(largely absent) adversaries:
from Jamaica, Nanny of the

Windward Maroons, Cudjoe and
Accompong who forced the English
to sign treaties; in Mexico,
Yanga and the town of San Lorenzo
de los Negroes; all the *palenques*
of Cuba; in Hispaniola, le Maniel;
the Bush Negroes of Suriname;
the many *quilombos* of Brazil,
including the Black Republic
of Palmares. And so on....

3

Although for hundreds of years,
we were trying to stay hidden,
wanting nothing more than to be
left alone, to live in peace,
to garden, I've found
no matter what you were
recording of plantations and
settlements, we could not be
omitted. We are always there
like some dark stain in your
diaries and notebooks, your
letters, your court records,
your law books – as if we had
ambushed your pen. Now I have
time to read (and garden), I who
spent so many years in disquiet,
living in fear of discovery,
am amazed to discover, Colonist,
it was *you* who feared *me*. Or

rather, my audacity. Till now,
I never knew the extent to which
I unsettled you, imposer of order,
tamer of lands and savages,
suppressor of feeling, possessor
of bodies. You had no option
but to track me down and
re-enslave me, for you saw me
out there as your own unguarded
self, running free.

ADVICE AND DEVICES

Gardening in the Tropics can be
quite a struggle if you don't
know what you're doing. When I go
to the agricultural fair, every
one there comes crowding round
to see my prizes. Even the ones who
take advice from the government man
and use a whole heap of sprays
and fertilize out all the taste
from the pumpkin and yam.

When they ask my secret I just
smile and say: Live Right and
Do Good. That's true, for the
world out there is full of hellish
creatures threatening to undermine
you, like cutworms and ants, but
the worst ones are the bad-minded
two-footed wearing pants, who will
do things to harm your garden or
steal your crop – unless you know

how to make them stop. Listen
to me (and don't tell anybody):
Once you find the right spot
for your garden, before you fell
a tree or pull a weed, be sure
to ask pardon to dig, with a
sprinkling of rum for Mother Earth's
sake (you should also take a swig
and rub some over your head
in case there's a snake).

Then, as soon as you lay out your
field, plant at the four corners
Overlook Bean to be your eyes when
you cannot be seen. Should the
evil-doers still trespass (for even
Overlook Bean has to rest) be sure
to burn wangla (but not to excess).
With the ashes, mix a trace of the
dirt from their footstep with powdered
hummingbird wings (for they never

stop beating) and Oil of Compellance
with six fresh leaves of what
some call Bizzie-Lizzie and we call
Impatiens. Wrap up in Cowitch,
tie with Chaini Wis and bury
at the four corners under the fence
at the exact commencement of the
new moon. The next time someone
(though we all know who) should
take pass and come into

the property to commit offence,
his foot-bottom, his whole body
will start to itch and tremble
and that culprit will have no
recompense, but be forced to
wander the earth, scratching.
After that, your patch will
thrive, for the Lord likes *you*
to deal with the covetous
so *He* can smile on the righteous.

There are other recipes and devices
to use for protection but my main
advice is: never explain,
especially to those who rely on
the plan of the government man
with the book. They are the
chief ones in need of your wisdom,
for their fields (with
all that fertilizer and spray)
will never stay healthy.

All I will say (when people
ask how my garden can bear
so, year after year without
wearing thin): you must know
what you're doing. For instance,
certain crops will only grow
if planted the first night of the
full moon, others should be
planted when the moon is waning.
There's a right way of doing

everything. Take pumpkin. The
morning you plant it, plan
nothing else for the day for
once you put the seeds in the
ground and water, you must stay
at your yard, lie down and rest
– unless you want your pumpkin
to grow worthless and run around
with no time to settle down and
bear. And when the vine is nicely

blossoming, ask a pregnant lady
to walk all over it to make the
fruits set and grow full, like
how she's showing. I don't have
to tell you plants won't thrive
if you're quarrelsome. Sometimes
I go to my fields and sing. The
birds join in and we have a real
harmony going. I keep the crops
happy, treat them right, so

they'll put out their best
for me to take to the agricultural
fair and madden everyone there.
I don't worry about bad-eye and
jealousy for I have nutmeg in
my mouth; in my pocket, rosemary.
When they ask me for my tips,
I take a deep breath and come
right out and say: Just Live Right
and Do Good, my way.

MYSTERY
African Gods in the New World

MARASSA: DIVINE TWINS

Our coming itself
was a miracle
One spirit split in two
equals one

We grow
We are fed
We sleep
We wake up
We play:

I am day you are night
You are left I am right
I am up you are down
You are young I am old
I am man you are woman
You are death I am life

– Let's play it again
the other way round

– The way it is
in the mirror?

Don't worry, Mother, sleep tight
Our spirits guard your hearth
We do nothing by halves
We are your ancestors
We are your children.

OBATALA: FATHER OF WISDOM

Unblemished
Father of Wisdom
Lord of High Mountains:
Take my aspirations
beyond heights
of great men
reached
and kept.

OSANYIN: GOD OF HERBALISM

One-legged man
shoots up a tree
root without end
his bird
of a voice
pitched perfectly
to forward our prayers
rain heavenly leaves down

O forest
O doctor
I halloa thee
my voice as tiny
as beat of bird's wing

You know what I need

      one leaf for sorcery
      one leaf for prophecy
      one leaf for healing
      one leaf for the pot

O wilderness
O harmony

Who says
one hand cannot balance
one leg cannot dance
one eye cannot witness
one ear cannot divine

the permutations of the leaves?

OSOSI: GOD OF HUNTING

The Master of Animals
waits for game

Meantime
he schools himself to discern the logic of signs
        in animal footprints and excreta
tracks constellations across the sky to establish
        the pattern of seasonal migrations
searches for extraordinary vision in plants
        expresses their juices in arrow and fish poisons
unravels the tongues of birds hoping to learn the
        secret names by which to summon them
transports his thoughts great distances into traps, asylums,
        cages, to learn ways of refining the hunt
duels with lightning to improve his speed; walks
        in step with the tortoise to learn patience

Sometimes
while waiting
he grants us the boon of attaching our prayers to his arrows
and he practices shooting
at stars.

OGUN: GOD OF IRON

1

Hand a' bowl, knife a' throat

our sacrifice dispatched
OGUN EATS FIRST

2

Iron in the blood feeds
your red-hot energy, fires
your metallurgy in the
cauldron or smelter,
transmits your power
to the forge, transmutes
carbon into diamonds,
expresses oil from rocky
strata, bends the centre
of gravity to your sword.

For the kill, you arm
battalions, beat
ploughshare into gun,
unleash atomic energy,
distil power from the sun
to shape our potential
for death or – if you
choose – life, for power
is your calling and
manifest its ways:

You forge our
connections, you fashion
our handshakes, our
friendships you seal,
bind our oaths sworn
in blood; for the life
of the spirit is fuelled
by fire engendered where
our heartbeats
spark into life.

Yet, heavenly transformer
of our weak impulses,
you allow our fevers,
the fire in our loins
our burning desires
to consume us
while, knife in hand,
iron-hearted warrior,
you coolly
stalk alone.

SHANGO: GOD OF THUNDER

He come here all the time
sharp-dresser
womanizer
sweet-mouth
smooth-talker
– but don't pull his tongue
is trouble
you asking
his tongue quick
like lightning
zigzagging
hear him nuh:
I SPEAK ONLY ONCE!

He well arrogant
is true but don't question
take cover
when his face turn dark
like is thunder
rolling
like is stone
falling
from on high
from the sky
is like rain

Just as suddenly
is sunshine breaking
is like water
in his sweet-mouth
again

Is so everything
swift with him
he don't stand
no nonsense (though
he likes to be
one of the boys)
he'll roll in here
on his steed
(plenty horsepower
there) ride in
like a warrior
of old (you expect
him to be waving
some primitive tool
like a hatchet)
When he comes in
no matter what tune playing
they rev up the drums
as if he own them
to play that zigzag
syncopated beat
that he like

Everybody rushing
to salute him
do his bidding
for there's no telling
the state of his mind:
I SPEAK ONLY ONCE!

The girls like him
(though they say
he have three wife already)
he sweet-mouth them yes
have his way
give plenty children

If they want him to stay
they must do as he say
he prefers
hanging around
with the boys
anyway
woman must know her place
plus he swear
is only son
he can father

I tell you something:
If you want
to get anywhere
with him
act
like you tough
that is what he respect
work yu brains
not sweat but cunning
win the fight
learn sweet-talking
be smooth

Just remember
he alone can strike
with his tongue
zigzagging
like lightning

Hear him nuh:
IS ONLY ONCE I SPEAK!

ORUNMILLA: GOD OF DIVINATION

Like St Joseph
the carpenter
taking our measure
sending back order
forecasting
forewarning
Foremost Diviner
how fortunate
for your children
what you have
ordered us forever
to recall: in
four-square
is all.

BABALU: LORD OF THE EARTH

Dogs herald your approach, Old Man,
the hot earth rises to greet you.

(We dare not fan, nor pray for cooler
weather though on our skin something

is breaking out and threading its way,
like beads). Lord, accept our offering,

our *vèvè* of grain placed outside
our gates to save you the pain

of that long walk in the sun-hot.
Spare us this time from visible sign

of our excess – the marks of your last
visit we wear forever on our skin

(with pride, we hasten to say, those
not yet put away in your cemetery).

Oh no, please don't misconstrue: for
whatever you send us, we thank you.

We thank you for the beads; we thank you
for the peanuts; we thank you for the

sesame seeds; we thank you for the gourds;
we thank you for the smallpox. And if

you do choose to come in, we pray you
find everything so spotless your broom

will not dislodge a single grain of dust,
for it would grow into such a whirlwind

(of pox, pestilence, plague) you'd sweep
the entire country clean – for which

- we hasten to say – we thank you; we
your children who are weak; we who are not

immune to invitation; we who cannot abstain;
we who have no restraint; we who succumb

so easily to temptation; for we know,
Doctor of the Poor, if you send affliction,

you also hold the power to heal us.

OYA: GODDESS OF THE WIND

You inhale
        Earth holds its breath
You exhale
        Cities tumble
You sigh
        We are born
You whisper
        The Hallelujah Chorus rises
You hiss
        Lightning forks
You sneeze
        Thunder rolls
You belch
        Oceans churn
You break wind
        Forests wither
You puff your cheeks out
        Bellows roar
You chuckle
        Angel-trumpets bloom
You enter the marketplace
        We trade glances
You whistle
        We dance
You sweep
        We fly
You yawn
        Death rattles.

Terrible Goddess,
no need to show your face.
As long as we breathe
we know you are there.

OLOKUN: GOD OF THE DEEP OCEAN

1

In the waiting room
beneath the sea
lies mythical Atlantis
or sacred Guinée

Who knows
save Olokun
master of the deep

guardian of
profoundest
mystery

2

Shall we ask him?

Shall we ask him
where the world tree
is anchored?

Shall we ask him
for the portal
to the sun?

Shall we ask the tally
of the bodies
thrown down to him

on the crossing
of the dread
Middle Passage?

Shall we ask him
for secrets read
in the bones

of the dead; the souls
he has guided
to his keep?

Will he reconnect
the chains of
ancestral linkages?

Send
unfathomable answers
from the deep?

3

Divine Olokun
accept the tribute
of your rivers

the waters of your seas
give back wealth
as you please

guard us from our innermost
thoughts; keep us
from too deep probing

but if we cannot
contain ourselves and
we plunge

descending
like our ancestors
that long passage

to knowing,
from your realm
can we ascend again

in other times
in other bodies
to the plenitude of being?

YEMOJA: MOTHER OF WATERS

Mother of origins, guardian
        of passages;
generator of new life in flood
        waters, orgasm,
birth waters, baptism:

> Summon your children
> haul the rain down
>
> white water: blue water
> The circle comes round
>
> Always something
> cooking in your pot
> Always something
> blueing in your vat
> Always something
> growing in your belly
> Always something
> moving on your waters

From Caribbean shore
to far-off Angola, she'll
spread out her blue cloth
let us cross over –

> Summon your children
> haul the rain down
>
> sweet water: salt water
> the circle comes round

Always something
cooking in your pot
Always something
blueing in your vat
Always something
growing in your belly
Always something
moving on your waters

If faithful to Yemoja
mother of waters, fear not
O mariner, she'll
smooth out your waves –

    Summon your children
    haul the rain down

    fresh water; salt water
    the circle comes round

    Always something
    cooking in your pot
    Always something
    blueing in your vat
    Always something
    growing in your belly
    Always something
    moving on the waters

Life starts in her waters
and ends with her calling
Don't pull me, my Mother,
till I'm ready to go –

Summon your children
haul the rain down

ground water: rain water
the circle comes round

Always something
cooking in your pot
Always something
blueing in your vat
Always something
growing in your belly
Always something
moving on the waters

Renewal is water, in
drought is our death,
we dissolve into dust and
are washed to the sea –

Summon your children
haul the rain down

white water: blue water
the circle comes round

Always something
cooking in your pot
Always something
blueing in your vat
Always something
growing in your belly
Always something
moving on the waters.

GUÉDÉ: LORD OF THE DEAD

By the sign of the crossroads
beat two turns of the drum
turn and beat again
put the pepper in the rum

lay out the cassava bread.
I might come. If I'm not busy.
Don't complain. You think
I'm just a trickster, playing

the cocksman, joking around
working brain. Remember: is you
waiting on me, not the other
way: today you here, tomorrow

you gone – if I say. Pray
I don't come dressed in top hat
and tails, dark glasses
on mi face, puffing big Havana,

strutting round the place.
If you realise what's good
for you no matter who else
you expecting you'll still

turn and beat the drum
put out the pepper rum, pile up
the cassava bammy, maybe a chicken
or two for company

and pray I don't get more hungry
than that

this very night.

TALKING OF TREES (1985)

> *like a root*
> *stopped by a stone you turn back questioning*
> *the tree you feed. But what the leaves hear*
> *is not what the roots ask.*

Martin Carter

HOMESCAPE

I was born with the knowledge
of mountains and solitaires
till jet planes and skyscrapers
seduced this to

mountains alone and one note
of the solitaire

till the politicians' words
reduced this to mountains

alone now the solitaire sings not
and knowledge is brittle
as glass

If the solitaire sings again
I'll be born to that life again

Alone I will walk through the glass

and become.

BIRDSHOOTING SEASON

Birdshooting season the men
make marriages with their guns.
My father's house turns macho
as from far the hunters gather.

All night long contentless women
stir their brews: hot coffee
chaklata, cerassie
wrap pone and tie-leaf
for tomorrow's sport. Tonight
the men drink white rum neat.

In darkness, shouldering
their packs, their guns, they leave.

We stand quietly on the
doorstep shivering. Little boys
longing to grow up birdhunters too.
Little girls whispering:
Fly Birds Fly.

COCKPIT COUNTRY DREAMS

I

In Cockpit Country
the hours form slowly like stalagmites
a bird sings
pure note
I-hold-my-breath
the world turns and
turns

I mountain goat plunged
headlong into this world
with eyes wide open
(dreaming so)
blinded by flame trees
and sunlight on river

green nurtured me

till mules turned circles round the mill
and large dark wings
like War

– Planes bringing bombs, said my father
– Babies, said my mother

(Portents of a split future).

II

Our road led to places on maps
places that travelled people
knew. Our river, undocumented
was mystery.

My father said: lines on paper
cannot deny something that is.
(My mother said: such a wasted life
is his).

III

Listen child, said my mother
whose hands plundered photo albums
of all black ancestors: Herein
your ancestry, your imagery, your pride.
Choose *this* river, *this* rhythm, *this* road.
Walk good in the footsteps of *these* fathers.

(Yet she could no more stop my mind slipping
those well-worn grooves of piety, work, praise
than rivers cease flowing).

Listen child, said my father
from the quicksand of his life:
Study rivers. Learn everything.
Rivers may find beginnings
in the clefts of separate mountains
Yet all find their true homes
in the salt of one sea.

IV

Now my disorder of ancestry
proves as stable as the many rivers
flowing round me. Undocumented
I drown in the other's history.

V

I had thought of walking far from the terrible knowledge
of flames. Spathodea. From ghost-ridden Trumpet Tree.
From personal disaster. God's blinding judgement.
Drunken mystery.

And whisps of smoke from cockpits crying lonely lonely.

But walking in the woods alternating dark with sunshine
I knew nothing then of cities or the killing of children

in their dancing time.

PRAYER

Pecharies
tackling the
hawks crying
in gunsights
casting
shadows

Keep these
from our door
spare us skyfall
except rain

Lord, let no
danger lurk
in Trumpet Trees
and Rolling Calves
be not true

children save
from early dying
casting shadows

Send a sign

let your glory
shine through clouds
beyond petcharies.

DROUGHT

This is no place for a
Christian man to
live in   the house
to a slight wind's tap
will give in

and tonight
the moon has a circle
round its eye the old
men say hard rain
will fall   let
the hard rain fall
if my fields go under I
will not surrender
in this place tender
shoots may yet arise

(and O bear this my
heart don't weep if
land is dear rum's
still cheap).

ANCESTRAL POEM

I

My ancestors are nearer
than albums of pictures
I tread on heels thrust
into broken-down slippers

II

My mother's womb impulsed
harvests perpetually. She
deeply breathed country air
when she laboured me.

III

The pattern woven by my
father's hands lulled me
to sleep. Certain actions
moved me so: my father
planting.

When my father planted
his thoughts took flight.
He did not need to think.
The ritual was ingrained
in the blood, embedded
in the centuries of dirt
beneath his fingernails
encased in the memories
of his race.

(Yet the whiplash of my
father's wrath rever-
berated days in my
mind with the inten-
sity of tuning forks.
He did not think.
My mother stunned wept
and prayed Father
Forgive Them knowing not
what she prayed for.)

One day I did not pray.

A gloss of sunlight through
the leaves betrayed me so
abstracted me from rituals.
And discarded prayers and
disproven myths
confirmed me freedom.

IV

Now against the rhythms
of subway trains my
heartbeats still drum
worksongs. Some wheels
sing freedom. The others
Home.

Still, if I could balance
water on my head I can
juggle worlds
on my shoulders.

TO MY ARAWAK GRANDMOTHER

Baptismal certificates are mute
while the whisper of a clay fragment
moves me to attempt this connection

I cry out
to you.

SEARCHING FOR GRANDFATHER

I

In Colón, I searched for my
grandfather without connection.
Not even the message of his
name in the phone book.

II

Along the line I found my
grandfather disconnected
at Culebra.
          Hacking at the Cut
he coughed his brains loose
and shook

(but it was only malaria).

You're lucky they said as they
shipped him home on the deck
of a steamer, his mind
fractured but his fortune intact:
Twenty-eight dollars and two
cents. Silver.

III

What he had learnt to do really
well in Colón was wash corpses.
At home the village was too poor
to patronize. He was the one
that died.

His sisters laid him out in a
freshly-made coffin and cried:
there was nothing left of the
Silver Roll to weigh down his
eyes.

For although his life had been
lacking in baggage, they didn't
want him to see that on this
voyage out he still travelled
steerage.

TOUCHSTONE

This is the only way for the mind
to wander: firmly balanced against the hoe
rooted in the earth, grounded
in the province of my fields.

The soil warms to my feet. I am based
in reality. Cannot stray too far become
a cloud dreamer. The grains of wood
score calendars in my hands.

My brown world below is stronger than
cloud in the blue.
Though the mind aches to know
the hand gripping a tool says: this is.

When passing birds tug at
my lifeline my head lifts. My feet
refuse to yield. The moment gone my life
goes slack again. Only my eyes water.

POLTERGEIST

where the dead are
separate from the living
by a thin veil only by a
thin veil the living
from the dead his mother
they buried late evening
on her grave they planted
Coffee Rose and a handful
of Resurrection lily

       his wife expected
something miraculous
when the lilies bloomed
like a man come to court
the daughter (hush she's
growing she's a woman now
beneath the gentleness
of plaits neatly rowed
there's a little soul
shivering hurricanes) and
mother sleeps under Coffee
Rose and a handful of
Resurrection lily

       easter day
just as the first stones crashed
into those thin walls,
and the pot lifted itself from the fire
a petchary picked up
the cry of that young girl

running down the stony
hillside with a fistful
of Resurrection lily
white and purple sprouting
miracles from her black hands.

HILL COUNTRY

The sun etches out the minutes of my days
under my dark eyes. The train, our only
regulation, shakes down the hours, stakes out
the limits of our lives
on this, my harsh and gentle island.

My ring finger tingles as my machete
flints on a stone. From far
hear my wife pounding cassava
in a cracked mortar singing
a cracked tune O
                    the futility
of crop cultivation in this place
the census takers never come. To whom
shall I marry my daughter?

Sons, too young to help, too old
to be not-born, too precious
to have seedlings feeding on your dreams,
Fist this red clay in your hands
hold the red gold, I tell them.
But I look into their eyes
and no gold comes, no dreams
arise and I know
this is merely the red clay
of a broken hillside and the parakeets
sit on the cedar stump waiting
for the young corn to ripen.

The sun cuts an arc on the housetop
the day goes by

my thoughts tremble on the edge
of something undesirable
my wife sings still
the sunbaked questions of our lives...

The sun marks the minutes, the train
the hours. Among the yam vines
and the trumpet trees we need
no clocks, no timepieces, no time
for the hunger in our bellies tells us
which way a clock's hands should go.

The train pulls home the day
draws it into citylights on two
black parallels. Later,
when my sons discover the agonies
of leached hillsides
it will pull them too.

They'll weigh down these memories
with a stone.

EIGHTH BIRTHDAY

The morning was trustworthy
routine tasks kept us anchored

at my party the children
keeled over in gusts of laughter
unchecked

late afternoon
the sounds receded as they left

beached once more in silence

I wept

who knows through what newly opened crack
this hurt crept?

PORTRAIT

Psychiatrists
could name the experience
but you merely
lived it, not yet
beyond temptations
crystallized
in a sugar bowl

Home
was where grannie
or ma lived but
no further than
down-the-road

Times
a bogeyman chased you
with a grinning machete
but safety lay
in warm laps
and cool arms until

Father

filled the doorway.

All this
as you stir with the
dog's stick
the dirty puddle
mirroring a face
half-past childhood.

The house no more now
than this fragment.
That dark-filled doorway
all that remains
to frame still

Your life.

ONE NIGHT, THE FATHER

One night
the father
split
a house
in two
one side
the only
sound the
mother
weeping
weeping
the other
riccochet
of bullets
butchering
banana leaves.

One night
the father
held them
in a state
of siege.
Furniture
loomed
barricades
against
the door
as in
war lore
each child
thought:
this bullet

is meant
for me.

One night
the neighbours
said a
drunken brawl
is all
the mother
shouted
an obstinate
No.

When the father
spent the bullets
for them he'd
also spent
himself.
Came
like a dried
canestalk
trashed
by hooves
of obstinate
mules
turning
the cane mill
round
round
till the day
the father
finally
broken
became
part of
that ground.

CHILDHOOD

Rivers flow red and swollen with the clay
of upstream mountains where the
rains fall. Mockingbirds call
in the woods from the roseapple tree
echo the cry of crazy-lost children
and the bird-filled hills fear still
sudden death. By slingshot.

The dead in a certain graveyard
cannot rest again after a long ago
awakening when Sunday School children
hunted cashew nuts on the way to church
and wept over penny-for-the-collection-plate
lost in the cracks of the tombs.

At the river Job's Tears wait still
eager hands seeking treasure
for stringing and logwood blossom boats
float far as Falmouth – or China – bringing
a fleet of magical ships to all
lingering downstream. The day
could turn magic. From the river
tables rise and rivermaids comb
their hair golden in the afternoon
singing.

COLONIAL GIRLS SCHOOL

For Marlene Smith MacLeish

Borrowed images
willed our skins pale
muffled our laughter
lowered our voices
let out our hems
dekinked our hair
denied our sex in gym tunics and bloomers
harnessed our voices to madrigals
and genteel airs
yoked our minds to declensions in Latin
and the language of Shakespeare

       Told us nothing about ourselves
       There was nothing about us at all

How those pale northern eyes and
aristocratic whispers once erased us
How our loudness, our laughter
debased us

       There was nothing left of ourselves
       Nothing about us at all

Studying: *History Ancient and Modern*
Kings and Queens of England
Steppes of Russia
Wheatfields of Canada

       There was nothing of our landscape there
       Nothing about us at all

Marcus Garvey turned twice in his grave
'Thirty-eight was a beacon. A flame.
They were talking of desegregation
in Little Rock, Arkansas. Lumumba
and the Congo. To us: mumbo-jumbo.
We had read Vachel Lindsay's
vision of the jungle

       Feeling nothing about ourselves
       There was nothing about us at all

Months, years, a childhood, memorizing
Latin declensions
(For our language
 – 'bad talking' –
detentions)

       Finding nothing about us there
       Nothing about us at all

So, friend of my childhood years,
One day we'll talk about:
How the mirror broke
Who kissed us awake
Who let Anansi from his bag

For isn't it strange how
northern eyes
in the brighter world before us now

Pale?

NANSI 'TORY

This is a story
of the man who was bought
in Africa/Guinea gold
brought as cargo
in the hold
All that crossed with him
his shit/seed
and a bagful of memory

(his heart
he ground into
powder left hidden
behind
a remembrance tree
on the beach
near Koromantyn/Elmina)

Landing
they emptied the hold

where the shit fell
grew luxuriantly
fruits of Africa/New World
akye, aloe, adrue and
compellance weed

the man
they sold

(Sweet sugar cane/sweet
remembrance)

For the rest of
his life
he was sure
he had died
in that
stinking
white hold.

But since this
is a story he
grew up to be
somebody's
grandfather.

One day
under pressure
from a child
who incessantly cried:
Tata, who we be
Where we come from?

he

re-

luct-

ant-

ly

let

go

his

hold

"Once upon a time ..."

Anansi
leapt from the bag

Heaven's doorkeeper
laughed
(after that
Jack Mandora
grew stern)

An atomized
heart on a
beach
reassembled

Awaiting
return.

X

December that year started out
alright though I knew
my heart could tear easily
as tinsel.

On King Street watching the legless
beggar on wheels I
counted my fortunes.

But what's the use of legs if you're
burdened with a mind
rushing headlong into dark
endings said the shadow

That night exorcising terror I
offered you love you
called me jailor

The season prematurely ended.

Up north Christmas trees
quietly retreated to the
dark forests and the
long awaited baby

never came.

NATURE STUDIES I

The poet
deliberates obscurity
the poet's lover
embraces mountains

do not
write
life poems

the worm
will
hear you.

Make
a compass
of your mind

bisect

life.

Learn
from nature
(yes, trees
have scar
tissue)

learning

recoil
like ferns
inhabit

the snail's
shell.

The poet's lover
contemplates children
the poet
studies suicide.

Having practised
surrender
learn patience:

Apprehend, not
comprehend.
Trees, not
people

Like mountains
grow roots
fired igneous

from mountains
learn treachery
            every minute
each aspect
changes.

The poet's lover
contemplates leaving
the poet
makes mistakes
again
again

grieving

the poet writes:

how weep
when trees conspire
to align me
vertical
and all the time
mountains?

The poet writes
a life poem

the poem
self-destructs

the worm

devours
the mountain.

NATURE STUDIES II

I

Studying mountains
I would make myself
stubborn
as igneous
receptive
as rock
forgetting
        times
when hills
range soft
as water-
colours run
transluscent
rainfall.

II

Mountains
slip scar
baring roots
to the core
to grow over cover
a lifetime (callouses
covered my heart
in two weeks).

III

Hard like dogs or adolescents the mountains
range in packs there is no escaping them it's not
the mountains that move it's your perspective you laugh
forgetting how in the cockpits of my endless
voyagings and your landlocked imaginings
            I lost mine. O

what right have I to speak of you in the same breath
as trees or mountains when I could liken you to
something alien like prairies. Or ice.

IV

You can always claim
I haven't made it
to the peak.
Still cliff-
walking
one day
mountains
will come
clear
as mirrors.
My lessons learnt
I will reach
beyond you
walk through
to the point where
mountain roots
intersect

all life.

Genuflect.

EPITAPH

Last year the child died
we didn't mourn long
and cedar's plentiful

but that was the one
whose navel-string
we buried
beneath the tree of life

lord, old superstitions
are such lies

REVELATION
(for G. Beck)

This road
has such
corners you know
John Crow sharpen
knife and fork
for somebody

      you

coming blindly
round a bend
tumble
headlong

      into

a delight of children
singing
and the wisdom weed
sprouting
bank to bank.

SONG OF THE CAVE VALLEY MAN

Once upon a time chile
I was young and dreamy
sunshine came hanging
over the green pond
down through the water
sliced up the bottom
shivered the old moss
smiled the tiki-tiki

then my mother called me home
and the sun fell

Once upon a later time
starapples ripened
under a full sun
purple they hung down
married with oranges
in an old panya jar
it was such fruit we ate
we called it matrimony

then my mother called me home
and the sun fell

Once upon a long time
faraway child time
sunflowers talked to me
of Cave Valley flood
bamboo stalks sang to me
sang me to sleep there
where granadilla ripened
over my hot head

so it happened once to me
before the sun fell

House too frail to
brace against a
hurricane. Any
breeze-blow can
topple it, a child
can tumble over it.
Yet let people sing
of it. Was made
by these hands.

Hands untrained
to make like
aeroplane, know only
reaping cane, planting
grain. Let them
marvel at the wonder
of it. These hands
made this house.

FUNERAL SONG

You hide I'll come
seek you I'd cried
to a boy
like green
in a garden
but the flowers
that hide him
are planted too deep
the sky
they've appointed
his warden

I count sunflowers
hibiscus
and daisies
daisies
chrysanthemums
and roses

I'll be good
if you'll keep me
I'd said
to the boy
like life
in the park
but his lips
now are sealed
and his eyes
cannot open
consciencia
confused
with the dark

What kind of period is it
when to talk of trees
is almost a crime
because it implies silence
about so many horrors?

Bertolt Brecht

LETTER FROM THE LESSER WORLD

Friend of the cellophane world
– separate packets
of instant dreams
just add money
and mix –

Do not
O do not say
it is the sea only
that divides us
the sole disjunction
a continental drift
that despite earth's wrinkles
we remain
'true brothers'
that you understand
that you understand

You do not understand.

How can you in your
central-heated city know
how sunspots on unpainted
tin shacks
sliver my eyesight
shaft my mind
with their infinite
refractions?

The term 'lesser world' is taken from the title of a study, *Children of the Lesser World* by D.R.B. Grant et al (1980).

Friend,
you do not understand
sickle cell anaemia
or sleeping on pavements
as we cannot understand
Baseball Season
or Fall

We do not need
interstellar leaps
we want to shorten
distances between
hospitals

And though flies
might cover the fish
in our open marketplaces
that does not kill,
like napalm.

We remain
not yet processed
cellophane wrapped
and frozen stiff
ready to be bagged

Though Rand McNally charts us
You can hardly now locate us
For we've found
that we're still waiting
to be found

Even as we await that
Second Coming
(Dub Version)
cosmic disturbances
tremble the sea

our bellies rumble
cities tumble

earth shifts

new wrinkles

divide us.

CROPOVER

If all
were all
unordered estates
she'd find her
home in

but croptime
makes decisive
your separation

your eyes
lock
on the colour
of her skin

clarifying.

Once she dreamed that you
unlocked your eyes and she
walked in and all
was all
and even though you said that
she had planters' eyes
you recognized

in her
there is
no sugar.

But you
do not see her
you see her
planters' eyes

and she

no longer dreams
of Harvest.

You are still the one to sow
and she to reap

Black Blast

All is not all

her home
she finds
without tempering.

CONCRETE CITY

How can I root
where you've poured cement?
I need a blame of grass
to rest on lest I topple.
Watch: I'm likely
to float lightly
as kapok or dandelion
as the last leaf left
on a final tree.
Watch me
skittering
rattling
and shaking
like a cassia pod
in the wind.

Farewell
Head
Over
Heels
Farewell

MADMAN AT TRAFFIC LIGHTS

When the Eye
turns red
you know
snake
shudders
and goes
still again
as you
stride
out and
in and
out its
coils to
charm it
to do
tricks
for you
But fearing
dread-
ness in
that one
red eye
the snake
goes
thrashing
to sal-
vation
as the eye
winks
green
again

You
on the edge
of out
and in
you
barely
miss
the hiss
of death
again
Triumphant
you shake
rattles.

TO THE MADWOMAN IN MY YARD

Lady: please don't throw rocks at my window
because this is Holy House and God send you
to get all the moneylenders out drive the harlot
from the inner temple. Again. Please don't
creep up behind me when I'm gardening beg me
lend you a knife. A bucket. A rope. Hope. Then
threaten to ignite, set alight and consume me
for you are the Daughter-of-a-Eunuch-and-a-Firefly
sent to X-ray and exhume me.

Lady: This is nonsense. Here I am trying hard
with my Life. With Society. You enter my yard
dressed like furies or bats. Bring right into me
all the hell I've been trying to escape from.
Thought a Barbican gate could hold in
the maelstrom. Keep out the Dungle. And bats.

What you want? Bring me down to your level?
A life built on scraps. A fretwork of memory
which is garbage. A jungle of images: parson
and hellfire all that's sustaining. The childhood
a house built of straw could not stand. The man
like a roach on the walls. So you choose
out of doors. Or my garden.

Lady: As you rant and you shout, threaten
and cajole me, seek me out then debar me
you don't move me one blast: Life Equals Control.

Yes. Here is what the difference between us
is about: I wear my madness in. You wear yours out.

AND WHAT OF THE HEADLINES?

In a perfect
equilibrium
like snow
and silence
I await
your gentle
coming
– Calling
of voices
across
silence –
Beyond the vapors
of your breath
other voices
calling
       calling
across
delinquent fences
from the gutters
of the all-night
streets
My anxieties
are
fanned
alive.
Last night a girl screamed.
Thirty-eight shutters
flew shut. Everyone
watched television
until it was
all over.

This morning they
wash blood from the streets
making virgin paths
for early risers
          – the knife
          rose
          and fell
          rose
          and fell
          like the rhythm
          of your
          breathing
Now in the quiet dawn
you ask me
Why are you anxious
Why are you sad
Why mustn't we talk
Of Love?

The man downstairs needs music loud
to fill his head
The music is so white
any day now
it will snow and snow

already it is snowing
on TV screens across the nation. Soon
it will snow

      red in the lane
where the shoe-less unemployed
nine-to-five faces grow and grow

In the concrete yard I
will a crack to open wide
invite a Kingston Buttercup inside
nothing's tougher – than the janitor
with weedkiller and

      the lane where
the school-less unemployed
nine-to-five faces grow and grow

Upstairs the lady preoccupied
with makeup and her boyfriend's wife
(tells her to get out of her life)
asks: who do these women so?

I only know
the Kingston Buttercup retreats
far underground for snow keeps falling
on television screens across the nation

while (in Living Colour)
the school-less unemployed
nine-to-five faces grow and grow

GREEN PARAKEETS

What is so wrong with a
universe where
every evening
precisely at six
from the west a flash
of green parakeets
angle my vision

there is such certainty
in this event when the parakeets
wheel I turn with them

(Months later)

Now the guns rage again
from the west a flash

every evening
precisely at six

looking through the cage
of my louvres
my vision shrinks
to a universe that is null.

ALBERT STREET

Rain ceases
with the coming
of the children

all the tired streets now
are filled with children's cries

they skitter like leaves
down the afternoon streets
all the innocent streets
of the world

Alas

all this early promise
of sunlight remains
largely unfulfilled

in undeclared wars
this May-be generation
these Now-smiling children

will fall, like raindrops.

r
  a
   i
    n

rain   viet
fall   nam
  scatters   ese
   the   bamboo
    playing   trees
     children   provide
    with   frail
    the   cover
     cutting   from
     edge   the
    of   breeze
     r   from
      a   the
      i   green
       n   r
        d   a
       r   i
       o   n
        p
        s

```
              hiro
    s h i m a's  c h i l d r e n
       a l s o      p l a y e d
       u n t i l        w h i t e
          r              c
          a              a
          i              m
          n              e
```

trench town children play
trench town children play

    bullets hail down
    bullets hail down
    bullets hail down

CITY POEM

I

Now the afternoon crossing of back streets
brings the call of voices: *hello hello. miss. psst psst.*
but I cannot answer: The Age of Anxiety
alas, is still very much alive.

(And if you taught me to speak
with your words would I touch
could I reach beyond the collapse
of garbage cans in hungry streets?)

II

Wen de bulldoza come a back-a-wall
we jus pick up all we have an all
we have is chilren an we leave
Mavis doan wan leave Mavis aksin
why why why A seh Mavis
move fus aks question las
de ting out dere biggern yu
an it caan talk
so Mavis move to but is like
she leave all sense behin. Fram dat
all Mavis good fah is aksin
why.

III

Why
did you damage
the statue
of the National Hero?

Because I have plenty damage
inside me.
You want to see
my scar?

IV

Halfblue childhood shocks but these
didn't matter. All roads
led outwards and Home
was Mother. Then afternoons
went dark. Hunger
became Brother. The hazy future
shadowed the roads. Failure
was Father. A night flashed
steel cold, your life
went dark six feet under.
The only road led back home
where, I do not remember.

THE SCAVENGER

Peel head John Crow
sit upon stump
scouring the dump.

John Crow know this city find
carcass and body dog head and
foetus three day baby eyelid
and footstump hardly any food kind on
dump Brother Festus an his tribe
no grab dat already?

Peel Head John Crow
sit upon stump
scouring the dump

John Crow everywhere
John Crow know
John Crow hear

THE MOTHER

> Muma mi belly soon
> grow bed so small
> last night Uncle Paul
> bizniz with me
> didn't know till he done –

Hush yu mout little gal
have no right
talk such nonsense
how come yu so shurance
and force ripe. Uncle Paul
help with school fees
and dress say he like

– what go on
under cover

girls look nice when they go
off to school

> Muma no school today
> mi body a hot me. Mi
> head dis a grow muma
> beg yu no lash me

One night you even say
yu own father did try
O god pickney nowadays
so wicked and lie
Study books dem not story.
If you get heddication don't
have to be like me

As for that lazy bitch there the
one Mistress Marshall she going
get her comeuppance as soon as a done

she think I don't know when she
think I round back who she entertain
round front say is insurance they selling
don't know where she gone in her
prison-pon-wheel. Say I tief out
the rice. Say black people not nice

Who don't know it will feel.

And where Bobby eh? A just know seh is trouble
that boy done get into. Do nutten but walk
street keep company. Toyota have no right
pull up door at night call the boy out say is
business he gone on. What right boy that age
have with business and firearm (that he swear he
don't have).

O God but this town is a crosses.

THE LADY

At 12 Daimler Close Kingston 6 Armour Heights/
Mistress Marshall wakes late with a headache/ the
light hurts her eyes/ what with pills and the whiskey/
her mouth tastes like death

She must go to the gym/ to keep fit and trim/for
her husband who's cheating with a girl/ who's not
slim

Mistress Marshall calls Eunice/ bring tea and the
papers/ no one dead no one born/ that she knows of/
but she turns to page eight/ and it's just as she feared/
for the columnists say that the p.m. is failing/ the
country is falling/ the party is foundering/ the
people are restless/ and the prophets of doom are
predicting a crash/ you see what I mean Mistress
Marshall doesn't know/ why her husband so worthless/
to stay on in this place/ every night the black people/
just waiting to break in/ to rob kill and worse/ but
he'd have to shoot first/ no black man will get in/
except that time there/ before she knew better/
before Mister Marshall start courting/
big family and all/ his hair was so curly/
his skin almost white/ not like
hers/ but it improve now she stop stand in sun
at the bus stop/ at the seaside she cover
with kaftan and hat/ say her skin is so delicate/ it
peels if the sun rests lightly on it/ everybody
wonder how naseberry/ so easy to peel/ but they
don't wonder long/ her jewels are real

Mistress Marshall want to go/ every day there she
nagging/ want to go to Miami where everyone gone/
for her skin would improve so/ and in climate that
cool so/ her hair would grow straight/ and the shops
are full so with strawberries and crystal/ caviar and
silver/ real silks and satin/ cake mixes and corn flakes/
good brandy and whiskey/ ryvita and salmon/
mushrooms and gammon/ in short everything that a
human would need

and the damn servant classes/ dem all is a crosses/
where the hell is Eunice?

THE VICTIM

Bobby Curren alias Festus alias Gre Gre
never come home last night

Bobby Curren
tie up tight

two fingernail
and him eyelid gone
Bobby Curren wont
walk again
without toes

but who need that
or head

when you dead?

THE DISPATCHER

Jack Spratt
wake up feeling alright
after business last night
conduct satisfactory
his hand full a ring
and other ting
cant mention in public
like gun and blood dunny

his grannie
did beat him
with supple-jack cant done
boy so tough
never cry
Grannie say
is bad seed

Jack Spratt come to town
to make something of life
country boy dont know nothing
but hoe, learn so fast
bout contracting
move so high is Jack Spratt
control territory
three police and a
half-Chiney beas
that is secretary to big man in town
(have a wife that ripe
for the plucking like mango
or naseberry........)

Jack Spratt look so right
kareeba and shades
well spoken and bright
drive BMW in daytime
Toyota at night
flashing cheque book
and passport all visaed
to go, have a room
in the ghetto, apartment
on hillside where his neighbour
is first cousin to a Minister's wife
(She complain bout his stereo
but shut up when Jack Spratt
just sight her. Say
she sorry. He is perfectly
right to make noise
in the territory.
Is not true that she nervous bout him
and his idren but she leaving tomorrow
moving in with a friend.)

Jack Spratt call himself
many things. Public Servant.
Contractor. People who say
overpopulation is the greatest
curse of the nation should
give medal to Jack Spratt
for what we over-produce
Jack Spratt will reduce
with efficiency and dispatch.

Jack Spratt dispatch
thirteen. Police hold him
three time but not long.

In this country Jack Spratt
walk bout free for he have
the connection Jack Spratt
have ability Jack Spratt
have mobility have contacts
and contracts Jack Spratt
have the might and the right
to decide who sleeping
in tonight and who outside
in Hope River bottom
or in cold Sandy Gully.

How Jack Spratt fly
so high? Stay up there
so long? Jack Spratt see.
Jack Spratt know.
Jack Spratt nuh John Crow?

REACHING MY STATION

'you have reached your station
Descend.'
Ferlinghetti

I

Finding your way home again
the journey fits and starts
in tired railway stations. Finding
a landscape redrawn by pygmies
in your giant's eyes the people
shrivelled.

II

Pressed into Sunday clothes
and diffidence the old ones clutch
their one possession: pride
which cannot buy respect nor bread
but tans the hide against
the centuries' forgetfulness.
They know the ship of state
will never sail into their lives
and beach, disgorging centuries
of promises. Nor even data gatherers
reach to label them statistics.

The young ones sicken their eyes
reveal this knowledge: why plant
when in the towns you know
your youth itself commands a rent

from gangster-politician-businessman
– it matters not a cent, the market's open.
Through gun more powerful than birth
than brain than wealth than life itself
the empires of your mind expand
take shape. A fingertip exults
your bravery, focuses your rage
and cures your impotence.

Let those who count such gains
take note: this village
is industrious. The bloom
of young girls fade in yearly
harvesting. Children the only
crop. High yield confronts
the barrenness of their lives,
pays dividends: a meal ticket
sometimes rent, at best
old age insurance. A bumper crop
shores up tradition: the female's
meant to drop.

But mothers know the starkness
of these times: guns easier
to obtain than milk. The moon's
been conquered, the hospital
not yet – it's just as far
and alien. And if some die, God
meant it. God or a neighbour's
envious eye – don't fight it.
For those of us who must remain
alive our leaders teach us
to displace our hate
– and cannily survive.

III

Finding your way home again
the landscape's shrunken, your eyes
play havoc with your dreams
mountains are hills, oceans
reduced to streams.

Finding you cannot enter still
nor leave this world your life's
locked into. Nor even hope
to change but wander far with bits
inside like shrapnel. Who needs
a war to teach you pain when people
dying slow – or quick – absorb you
in the very cancer of it. Your face
reflects the railway station's
squalor your eyes the self-same
dying you cannot hide –

You have reached your station

Descend.

Or perpetually ride.

CHILDREN'S HOSPITAL

Look now the child
facing death. Who
will commute this sentence
to life?

Su-su
Su-su
Su-su

Once upon a time
there were trees on Parade

Trees on Parade?

Trees on Parade. Listen:

The Ebony trees are celebrating rain
Spathodea's lapping Kingston like a flame
On the western railing Scarlet Cordias burn
Casuarina weeps Laburnum's numb
And Woman's Tongue clatters out of turn:

Who hears this? Who sees this? And who knows?

1907 earthquake when churches fell down
Tamarind Tree swayed. But Banyan held firm.
Come. Let us sit under Banyan tree and
reason together. Like Prophets of old

or the Big-tree boys
of old Kingston town

They baad
They tough

Like Ironwood
Lignum Vitae

Quick fe bus' yu head with a coco-macca stick
if yu jus' seh 'Feh!'

Feh!

Aaagh!

Oh Gawd. Let Ah lie down lie down lie down down
            down

Under Bullhoof. Bombax. Seaside Mahoe.

Sleep under

            Sissoo
            Sissoo
            Sissoo

Till Ah cool down.

Wake up bwoy!
Solja a come
Blood fe Blood
Fire fe Fire
Colour fe Colour
Ebony fe Ebony
Black fe Black
Mahogany Mahogany

Stop su-su gal
Solja give no quarter
Drop yu baggie dawta

Fustic stain their khaki
Mahogany stain their floor
Ironwood stain my life
From my Calabash break
Blood stain my –

     Baby
     Baby
     Baby
     Baby
     Baby

In Kingston some witnessed history
Turn the leaves and see:

W. Adolphe Roberts saw the funeral of Madame
        Caesar the noted Haitian voodoowoman
Vic Reid saw the hard little streets dripping their toes
        in the sparkling blue water
A Gleaner photographer saw Bustamante bare his
        chest to the police guns
Queen Victoria saw everything but is saving it for
        later

Green was our rage once
Harder than Almond

Blood fe Blood
Fire fe Fire
Colour fe Colour

Our roots tied up the harbour

Mangroves of resistance.

Cane trash mi life
Cane break mi spirit
Cane sweeten mi bizzie
Banana rotten mi clothes
Stone-bruck mi womanhood
Cargo strain mi muscle

Police baton bus' mi head

    Strike
    Strike
    Strike
    Strike
    Strike

Now what can we create behind fences?

Deadwood
Holes in the Ground
Towers of Concrete
Bridges of Loneliness
Twigs of Derision
Corollas of Sadness
Flowers of Suspicion

Up the road from Bellevue
I sing I-song
When Sandbox explode
Release me
Jerusalem Thorn crown me
Almond nurture me
Guango shade me
Cordia ban mi
belly an' bawl it out ya. No more

     Su-su
     Su-su
     Su-su

But the pages are scattered
The leaves are all fallen

Cassia
Poinciana
Poui

How shall we record then, my
Orphans of Dustbowls?

     baby
     baby
     baby
     baby
     baby

In our silence reaping
Duppy Cherry heritage
Yokewood birthright
Let us roll in the Dustbowl
and kick up our heels

    Sissoo
    Sissoo
    Sissoo

EYED
NEW AND UNCOLLECTED POEMS

'With my little eye, what did I spy?
All passed through my mind then
like thread through the needle's eye
for nothing was I ready to see.'

'With my little eye…', Over the Roofs of the World

FABULOUS EYELIDS

Et nos parpières fabuleuses. O
(And our fabulous eyelids O)
St-Jean Perse, Éloges 2

O ma mère, Madonna of the clothes-line
Embrace me, the child cries.

                    Stiffened against
the breeze, braced against the sun in her
eyes, Madonna the vise grips clothes pins
in her mouth, jabs the line, nappies
endlessly slapping white clothes Jesusing
to blue skies
                  and khaki pants for sons
1, 2, 3, 4, stiffening in the breeze with
father's workingman's blue that wouldn't
do for Sunday sporting that she pretends
she doesn't know about though she adds
more and more blueing to his whites nicely
ironed for the village rooster's outing.

One day, the sport was left on our doorstep.
She took her in, grudgingly.

                  O sister, my sister of the
fabulous eyelids unlocked, you have our
father's eyes. I took your hand. With you,
our house at once grew.

In the wash, increasingly, much too much blue.

EYE WASH

The Grandmother altering clothes to fit the child
sings until she pricks her finger on a pin. Stops
singing. Holds out the finger with the drop of blood:
Says: *You see this? Tis the sign of your ungratefulness.*

The room of highly polished mahogany furniture
is slowly filling up with tears.

EYE-WATER

Railway station in the mist
Dawn is breaking
I'm barely as high as the dewdrops on the grass
Bound for another place
My heart heavier than my suitcase.

EYELET/AIGLET

You know the old woman who lived in a shoe?
Got the occasional windfall and used it to buy laces.
She kept one against hard times and she made each child
take one eyelet and thread the lace through. To teach them
the virtues of cooperation – and claustrophobia.

Children, children! Wouldn't you rather be an aiglet –
the tube at the end of the shoelace – swinging free?

OUT/IN

Let cooling breezes blow, like mother's breath
on the thumb you crushed in a closing door.
Remember always (she didn't say) that
men will leave and women will stay to tend
the fires and bank their passions. Until the day
she ran away with a fire extinguisher salesman.
When my father too walked out that door
I came to like possession of a finite space
to keep my heart a spotless waiting room.
You might have heard of me, called
Miss Haversham or Penelope.
In this place though, I'm one of the Barrel
Children: the ones who pace to measure
the emptiness displaced by foreign treasure.

So-called 'Barrel children' in the West Indies are those whose parents have emigrated and whose only contact is often through the barrels of goods they send them.

SURE SHOT

And the child age 10 leans over with her cell phone camera
to take a picture of her classmate in the coffin
and a picture of the child taking a picture of her classmate in the coffin
(draped with a cloth reading: *Stacey-Ann Gone Too Soon*)
ends up on the front page of the newspaper. Of what use is that?
Is this grieving when the leave-taking is a moment for shooting
a picture of the dead child who wasn't dead a month ago
when she was caught in a crossfire and a single shot laid her low
brain dead in a hospital bed while the picture freezes and the shooting's
still up in the air. Where do we go from here? What can we say
when the fashion pages display models getting smaller and younger every day.

The camera doesn't lie. So many shots per minute. Automated. Digitized.
Worlds can be broken, blown to pieces in the blink of an eye.

Yet some old-fashioned curating refuses to die.
We all end up in a dark room. Forever.

KILLER BEES

This is not a pretty picture. This is a picture of a girl
pushed to the edge by a wedge of her schoolmates.
This is a crowd shot, a loud shot of laughter and hate.

What is the scent, the flower that blooms inside of her
that attracts the killer bees?

WHITE NIGHT

'Green is the supreme luxury of the Moscow winter.'
Walter Benjamin

He wakes *not half as beautiful* as he could have been
had he been other
Dried claws of matted grass imprint his face
his bed a slap of cardboard on the once green park

The man last night in the white Mercedes
could have been black like the earth
or white as the Russian winter, or other

The boy like a flower could *outshine everything*
if he could
if he would
dream of something like *spun sugar*
with *which the tongue indemnifies itself*
against the bitter

If he could he would get a job selling to motorists
at traffic lights *flowers with the heads of saints looking out*
among them or *spun sugar* sweeties made by a granny –
coloured coconut drops and candy bump and peppermint
sticks and *marzipan flora*

But there was no lock on the door of home and
he'd lost some marbles, so fate fixed
his livelihood to being drawn and quartered
like the flag that flies from
the Heroes section in the park.

And the only flower is his youth that starts out
oiled and erect and muscular like Blue Mahoe,
the National Tree's flower,
that swiftly changes from orange to crimson
to the limp scarlet of decay
in just one night and day.

Beneath their ornate monuments
the National Heroes weep and say: we never knew
the promise of green was *the supreme luxury*.

Another night of trawling
with the boy as *candy-icing*

and wild-eyed cannas making witness statements
as convincing as *bunches of artificial carnations*
in a *Moscow winter*.

A 'found' poem, with some words (in italic) extracted from Section 11 of
Walter Benjamin's essay on Moscow (1927)

HURRICANE WATCH

Every year we are forced to reinvent ourselves, growing shabbier. Perhaps uncertainty comes from the shifty breath of Hurricanes, their unlocked eyes revolving always counter-clockwise. Watchful. Unmaking us.

'WARNING: KEEP AWAY FROM THE CLIFFS'

This sea needs no warning for it is born every morning
like pewter that needs cleaning/All that tells me it's alive are
the noisy hunter gaulins/ and the ripples on the tide/ This sea
is always hungry for whatever breaks its surface/ and though I
know it knows what I will never know/ I'll stay anchored here
in green/ I would never dream/ of diving/ for the horizon /is
a dread straight line/ And the ways of the sea/ are conniving/

CRUISE SHIP LEAVING PORT AT NIGHT

Full moon and wine and leaning over the railing
    imagining a time when other watchers from the shore
        gazed on this very sea five hundred years and more ago
            as strangers floated in on galleons golden in the moonlight

when, suddenly, to my right, a sight such as that one: a cruise ship leaving port,
    afloat in a sea of light, golden in the moonlight. I was as awestruck
        as those earlier watchers from the shore must have been,
            except that my galleon was leaving

and the sea and sky, my heart, were not left empty and bare-faced and blasted.
    For the fleecy clouds continued to scud across the marvellous,
        star-studded sky, the little waves gambolled like Biblical lambs.
          And I was left with the land that was still mine.
          At least as long as the wine and the full moon lasted.

DEAD STRAIGHT

I'm travelling back home to you but it's an omen:
my road map's creased and torn along dead straight lines.

The hill and gully ride is over now and I'm flat out
on the dead straight highway with a toll.

Not a glimmer of the coastline as I try to make it home
to you through a forest of hotels as thick as thieves,

for the sea, the coves and beaches once seen through
seaside shacks and palm trees have been sold,

and the rest of us are herded to the verge by this new
highway, while over there our beauty is extolled,

bottled and sold. And gated. In this new paradise,
the only palms are greased, and somebody's beach umbrella

has replaced the shade tree we once sat under and the
towns and settlements moulder as they are bypassed.

I can no longer witness on this highway with a toll that makes us
seem as modern as elsewhere. For elsewhere

is not where I'm meant to be. And a dead straight
highway leaves no scent, no monument to the past,

no scenic beauty for the curvature of my eye to take in.
And endless empty space is not inviting.

But perhaps there's no social meaning to this tirade, after all.
I'm just feeling lost without a map as I make it home to you

and pay the toll. You could see it simply as a love song
to the curving of your cheek bones, to the mountains

of your thighs, the hill and gully passion of your eyes, and your hair
that is not dead straight but very much otherwise.

GUAVA JELLY SCORE

Me running across the yard
just as Aunt skimmed guava froth from the bubbling pot
and tossed it. Never to remember the arc of the boiling syrup
that curdled my skin; their cutting the clothes from my body,
the screaming.

I was four, I always say. I don't know
if I was happy before that day.
Later, I remember, though.
After the daily dressing at the hospital,
standing alone for hours by a window
in an upstairs room in a house in Montego Bay,
incubating a deeper wound: wondering
when the floor of the world had begun to sway,
why the nearby sea was drifting so far away.

For years they rubbed cocoa butter
on my corrugated skin. It erased nothing.
I loved guava jelly and forgot to ponder
how something so smooth, so sweet,
could score so deeply under.

GREEN BUSH GREEN BUSH GREEN BUSH

Behind the hills at evening time the sun fell down
the landscape weeping for a song
Whatever made you blue was never said
and children's voices greeted every dawn.

Years later you spoke of praying for relief
of daylight and from shame you could not name.
And how you foolishly invoked the mantra:
Green Bush Green Bush Green Bush

which in the open light of day worked every time.
You were the one that most feared wasps
yet you were never stung. Your invocation
always kept you safe.

Telling us this in fragments now it is our eyes
that sting. There was no help for it. Whatever balm
you summoned never came. 'All that foolishness
they filled us up with', you wistfully complain

of parents alive and dead. 'And yet... and yet...
when all was said and done, you couldn't go
to anyone.' To remove it (you didn't say). The sting.
The festering. To plaster it with three green bushes.

Green bush green bush green bush is a Jamaican children's charm against
wasp stings. If stung, the application of three green bushes picked at
random is supposed to ease the pain.

At last I understood your lifelong bitterness.
He hadn't died as wasps are said to do when once
they sting. He kept on stinging. Protected
by the charms of sweetness that he stole from you.

GRAND-DAUGHTER LEARNS THE ALPHABET

I myself had learnt the alphabet once,
long ago. In a place that was small
and known. But my forgetfulness has grown.

Here, your marks on paper scratch at my heart
as if they were the dragon's teeth sown,
that split our tongues, that made us scatter.
That made me forget myself, my own alphabet.

I'm a poor guide but I want to erase those scratches,
wipe the slate clean. I'm handing you over
so you can go to places that I have never seen.
Its magic leads you on, doesn't it?
These hooks that pull the sounds fresh from your mouth
and place them in your fist.

HOOK

The woman is standing on the pier leaning over.
    Her hands trace lines to the water.
        It's become a habit with her, this wandering
        off from Bellevue to seek a face that fillets
        her eye-water: that of her daughter,
            who set out long ago to make her own big catch.
        From another shore she sent a line or two, now and then.
            Enough to hook her mother so that absence becomes
                the present of a dress she made for that child
                            wish you could see it
                            white pique polka dots on blue
                            with a swiss lace collar and
                            a fastener at the back that a mother
                            must unhook so the child can take off
                            her one good dress before she lies down
                            to rest. But you see my trial now, ee?
                            Just look at this don't-care girl
                            that wearing her one good dress
                            there in the water when she must know
                            is still her old mother with the arthritis
                            who must hackle up herself so bend over
                            and tackle this rusty ol' hook and
                            eye fastener.

THEY'RE STONING THE MANGO TREE AGAIN

They're stoning the mango tree again.
Puny fruits and leaves shower down like rain.
The best of the crop has retreated to the top
of the tree and out of reach and no one
dares to breach the rampart of ancient trunk
and limbs armed with spiky wild pines
and stinging ants. Still they come, the army
of mango scavengers, with sticks and stones
and the heavy artillery of the fallen branch.
The bottom half is nearly bare of fruit now
and the reapers grow increasingly frantic.

Get a life I want to yell at them. Or, *find
another mango tree. If this one were to
charge for her services, with so many
solicitations all day long, she'd be filthy rich.*

Instead, from my window I have the last
laugh. As soon as the reapers have vanished
for the day, the feathered residents
come to stay. Soon I'll hear over and over
the BIF-BOOF sounds of mangoes dropping
from the topmost limbs and hitting the ground.
Ripe mangoes laughing and rolling around.

By tomorrow when the reapers return to
retrieve this fallen treasure, the birds,
the wasps, the flies and the worms
would have dined at leisure.

CHRISTMAS PUDDING

I didn't have a child's heart, I swear. Each year
as Christmas drew near I drew further into myself
wanting to creep into the huge old ceramic jar
on the shelf and drown in the aroma of pimento
and clove and dried fruit marinating in rum.
Wishing Christmas would never come.

But Christmas came alright and the one part I liked
was the making of Christmas pudding.
It started on the day they took that jar from the shelf,
bustled around to fire up the Calidona Dover
wood-burning stove, grease the cake tins
rub up the sugar and butter in the mixing bowls
throw the sifted flour and the beaten eggs
and the orange peel and the candied citron
and the rose water and vanilla essence and
the whole jar of drunken fruit in.

The puddings couldn't wait for the date, the 25th,
O no, the cooks wouldn't hear of it. Christmas
Puddings have to be baked or steamed at least two
weeks before the event. Then, quietly sitting
in their tins, soaked again in good over-proof rum.
THAT'S THE LAW. At least of pudding-shaped
cooks who would never go around arresting drunken
men for imbibing too much of their Christmas pudding.
O no. Not content with that alcoholic haze, on the day
they add brandy to the pudding and set light to it. I swear!

And I know swearing is a bad habit. But it's not
my fault. It came from lifting the lid of that old
crock and inhaling even before the cooks got hold of
that rum-soaked fruit each year and drowned it.

COUNTRY FUNERAL

Your funeral was a bit of a circus.
No surprise since you were the
ringmaster type, able to crack the whip
but not too proud to play the fool.
Too earthy to be an aerialist, you
sank gracelessly to the ground.
The minute you were decently covered
your children took down the blue tent,
swept up your black-clad widow
and flew. You alone pegged steadfast
to this mound.

Who will tend your grave? That is of
no consequence. You are where
you were always meant to be: in nature's
most intimate cell, exhorting the bursting seeds,
moulding up yam hills, comforting
tentative tendrils. Unravelling the tangled roots
of vines to discover the secret of how
water walk go a pumpkin belly.

The neighbours look at me and say: 'her eye dry, ee!'
'she hard-hearted, bad', 'she never cry'.
Little do they know how I mourn:
one day I'll come around, put my ear to the ground
and cheer: knowing
the Master of Plants
is still working miracles here.

FLIGHT

(For John Harrison)

On your patio you were assembling the body of a
Pitts Special which made me tease you with
Bertolt Brecht's assertion: "'Man is no bird/No one
will ever fly' the Bishop said to the people."

This bird acquired wings painted bright blue. One day,
miraculously, it flew. There was no stopping you.

Years later – I never knew, for I had flown (the
prosaic way) – never knew the sickness that travelled
through you

with the speed of flight. Departure date only slightly
stayed, borne up by the old RAF fighter courage and
the music of Villa-Lobos.

From Up Park Camp Chapel, one last fly past (I
wasn't there). I gathered that you took off, soared into
the air over royal palm tree;

beyond Palisadoes you took to the open sea, just as the
voice of Victoria de los Angeles singing 'Bachiana
Brasileiras no. 5'

swooped to earth, bore down on the awestruck
mourners who rose standing in one last salute
to a perfect landing.

GREENHORN

anxious as a caterpillar wary as green lizard he steps into the garden
city boy in his slick shoes his heart locked up tight as artichoke his feet slipping
on wet grass his world still an oyster
the jaunty and unencumbered greens of meadow, woodland, prairie, rain forest,
savannah are extortionate to his eyes
nauseous he steadies himself by envisioning what he came to see: golf greens
and civilised lawns housing estates freeways shopping malls hotels

revitalised he opens his eyes and fails to register

The leaves turning and signalling to each other
The grasses sharpening their cutting edge
The green-eyed monster stirring
The emerald of Lucifer

PERSEPHONE

The dark lady in her garden tends her skeletal
trees, she's under the ground for this season.
It's cold and she needs the sparkle of fire
to warm up her body, prepare her green dress

for her coming-out party; she's starving
herself for a reason. Who knows when we see
her splendour in spring, the cost of this beauty?
The gossips who sing: She wears her clothes

well. O she always had beautiful bones. Do they
still tell of her husband the abductor (or has he
been redeemed?). Do they say how her mother's
extravagant keening endangered the world?

Of her complaints to her daughter of *i told you
so* and *i warned you of dark men of bright
flowers beware but even then when you were
small did you listen? o no, by impulse you*

always were stricken. The dark lady knows
(but she just doesn't say) as she crosses the
threshold arrayed in her finery: It's impulse
that sparks fire, starts the engine of growth,

drives the green fuse through the flower, sap
through trees, brings new verdance to the bower.
But at what cost to my lady? She grows weaker
by the end of each season in the sun, returns

to that dark room to rest. OH MY HEART (her
husband taking over from her Mum). HERE, DEAR,
TAKE THIS RED PILL. He opens the box, the door
of unknowing. One seed less, yet a thousand

still glowing. Again and again, she yields
to temptation for she's seized by both Eros
and mourning. The bright red interior opens
for him. Yet it's he who's been tricked. From

one seed new life's always growing. So her
triumph: Each year he allows her – briefly –
to escape the snare of the flower; walk
through that door and return to her mother

who – never to forgive that initial loss – is
forever glowering. Forgetful now, she leaves
her dress rumpled at times, her bed unmade
and sour. Says *the heat's worse than it's ever*

been. Says *the day he grabbed you was an*
evil hour. The dark lady endures it all for her
secret bliss: the fire she snatches from the jaws
of death to ignite springtime in the world.

Yet, beneath her green dress at her coming-out
party, who would guess how wildly her pomegranate
heart beats to return underground for a taste of
that treat: the fruit from the orchard of Death.

THE DROUGHT
for Velma Pollard

The seamstress started cutting the air with her scissors
for a tear in the sky, a rent in blue fabric.
The laundress aired out the clothes.
The optimist said: Look: no mosquitoes.
The teacher trawled the dictionary for a spell
The preacher condemned the wicked to hell
(which didn't bring down blessings from above).

The kids ran around dirty which suited them.
No one cried: wash your face, say your grace
before meals. People stopped thinking there
was anything to living, to give thanks for, except
the meticulous few who give thanks for
everything. Rock bottom was reached though
when the cook started using less water in the dough.

O
& O

The government announced it was the wrong kind of rain
for it refused to fall in the catchment area.
The pipes were locked, dogs tongued the last drops.
Nothing dripped. Everyone repented. You know the drill:
If it rains again I'll be a better person, I won't drink to excess.
I won't let taps drip or drips drop. Until, that is, there's water in
them again.

Nature gave up at that stage. The orange tree cut off her sap
to let her offspring drip dry. The fruit coughed and withered.
The farmer butchered the last of the cattle and drank its blood
on the sly

Oooooo
   & o
my

The fish in the pond stayed alive.
A miracle? Let's not quibble. Rainbow-hued
expensive ornamental fish were not ones to set on dish.
But as water became more precious than fish
each time a pail was lowered, a fish secretly
dived into it.

O –Oh.

Yes.

Oh!

When the drought was over (I assure you it was)
in the dried-out fish pond they found not the
smallest token of fish, not a bone, not a scale,
not a cartilage, not a fish head. Some said
it was a miraculous sign. The more fanciful
claimed the fish transubstantiated
into vapour that went up into the skies
and came back down again as rain (though some
would have been more convinced had that been wine).

I'm sworn to secrecy but I'll whisper what I know:
Why does the rainbow keep bending down low low low
to gaze in the dish of the pond, gaze and gaze
until the water shimmers into a kaleidoscope
of dazzlingly beautiful ornamental fish?

Huh?
Uh-huh.
Oh!

THE EYE OF EVERYTHING

'Death's needle looking for thread.....'
Pablo Neruda, 'Solo la muerte'

Death in our yard is a three-foot horse, a hearse
        is a discord, a terse way of life
        is a blanket of dread
        is a blood stain that's spreading and spreading
.

Death is a bullet with one name on it
But death cannot read
and death cannot count
and death comes rattling in with bullets for all
and death is five dead and
one blue note

death is the fire in the hut
the machete in the night
the toddler playing in the dirt
        on the pathway of revenge

Death rankles as the wound in the soul of the one
who was a no-name child just like this one
who left school without an A or an X
no certificate of belonging, of knowing who he is
or what he came on earth for.

Death says:
I would kill to know who I am.
My gun is my family
I carve my own bloodlines
I emblazon my names in the headlines.

Death is the needle looking for thread

Death is the engine that runs out of fuel
The early blooming flower that falls too soon
the light bulb that blows in the moment that's critical

Death is the pain without end, the crucible,
the chalk-marks on the floor
the galliwasps's gaze
the x of the cross
the cracks in the glaze
the hunt for a cure that runs out of steam
the closing of the door
the scorpion's sting
the malicious intent
the act of revenge
the lighthouse lamp that fails

Death is the out of in, the upside down,
the zag of zig, the turnaround

Death is the marrow in the meat
the matter in the spirit
the rumble in the street

Death stalks without fear or favour
death enters each life equally
death is the true democracy
better than the ballot at choosing randomly
or targeting if that's your preference
Death is the ultimate job seeker needing no reference.

Death is the needle looking for thread

Once death sat inside an enclosure
a monument to pride and achievement
a listing on marble of names and their good deeds.
But death knows death knows death knows
where the thread goes
                    Death could not sit long with
hypocrisy; walked over that fence and out of
that cemetery, shunned the hollow promise of
consecrated ground, walked into the town to seek
justice. To gather names to engrave on that house.
For a cemetery is only a dormitory

They say that duppy blessed with holy water
is the baddest duppy. And the ones that are bred
in the tombs of hypocrisy have
no conscience dog-heart.
Yet all will fall to the reaper.

Death is the needle looking for thread

In the cemetery the dead are laid out like the living,
the poverty-stricken, the nameless, still have their slums
the churchical lie together waiting for the revelator
the BIG MAN lies in his house of death
with wife and children: a bloodline. Shanties and mansions
together rest. The needle makes connections manifest.

Holes in the ground are houses too
for the victims that are nameless
but their eyes have registered you.
Who knows, who knows where the needle goes
looking for thread to sew up the lips of those
who give tips: the dead informers.

Death is the needle looking for thread

Death is lamentation, Ezekiel
and chariots of fire. Death is revelation
and horsemen travelling two by two or
in packs or in posses. In cars and planes and
trains, on foot, on camel, on asses. Death shall not
let them lightly pass. It snares or pricks whom
it chooses.

Death is the needle looking for thread

The thread that's a red, red line through history
that loops and curls and knots like a net
of discovery, entrapping pirates, bankers and
cutlass blades, planters whips and sinews
of slaves, politicians' lying tongues and the
rachet knife cutting the root of innocence,
the bullet's trajectory riding on collusion:
richman, poorman, beggarman, thief,
policeman, businessman, presidents and those
that preach. If any pass through thread's weave
as knots work loose, the thread will be dragged
by the needle of truth.

With wide open eye, the needle passes
through doors, through secrets, through lies
some might fall through thread's weave, some are
caught in the knots, thread makes no judgement
it is the needle that plots.

So, MAKE WAY! MAKE WAY!
Looking for thread, looking for thread
to bind up the wounds of the lost, the betrayed,

from the towers of commerce to the door of the church
to the shanties of the poor where the john crows perch
no parliament here only tenements of fear.

Sinnerman, there is no way out, no consulate.
Here one finds neither passport nor visa
only this vine here that looks like a sign there
like a thread to the exit of the maze of your life
and the bloodied signs you left on the way
your fingerprints netted as clear as day
as you pass through the eye of scrutiny.

If justice on earth has too wide a weave
the snare of the cemetery is tight like a sieve
like a noose, like the knot of judgement.

The needle will always find the thread.

POEM WITHOUT ENDING...

'So much things to say'
Bob Marley

I couldn't think of anything to say
that would soar above these treetops straight to you.
They're cedar trees by the way, not *juniperus*
but *cedrela odorata* used to make canoes
and coffins

              like the one I saw go past our house once,
a coffin shaped like a narrow clothes iron
borne on the heads of men who had imbibed
too much at the wake the night before.
They weaved untogether down our dirt road
like the belly of an accordion played by a madman
and my mother had to call me away
from the window because I laughed so much.
But I still peeped through the jalousie which is not
a misspelling for jealousy but a type of window
for holding secrets in. When the centipede-like feet
of the coffin took a sudden turn and wove towards
our house I ducked down with fear for in our part
of the world the dead are known to direct
the movements of the coffin bearers to the houses
of people with whom they have history.
No matter how hard the bearers pull
the dead pull harder towards a date with
destiny, envy, malice or debts to be paid before
its final disposition in the cemetery.
O could I (eleven years old) be the one guilty?
But when I stood up again, my knees still quaking,
I saw our family had been spared; the dead

was making the bearers dance in another direction.
The accordion wheezing faintly on cedar-filled air.

....

I didn't dance then because my mother said
it was sinful but that didn't stop that dance
when the cymbals rolled in church and the spirit
colonised my head.

....

What I've just said isn't true. I never got into
the spirit or spoke in tongues but I put it in
to make me seem more interesting. Like 'therapy'
or 'botox' or 'children'.

Their absence doesn't make me any less
proverbial.

....

Escaping from winter, flying into the sun,
flying from

embalmed landscapes below
hieroglyphs of cities etched in snow

how swift is our movement
above the straying clouds.

Still nothing to say that will bring us closer except:

The cloud doesn't know
its shadow keeps pace

Time is on the doorknob
that waits.

The clock doesn't speak without
the second hand

The padlock is useless
without its tongue.

. . . .

Nothing is certain here. Moonbeams
can scorch and owls fly backwards.
The garden is aflame with fireflies whose
lights burn cold and flame trees
turn awkwardly to the moon.

What can I tell you that would validate
my identity? Laundry flaps on the line like
pale hands of moths torn in the wind.
The sea in retreat exposes bitter knocks.
The needle is still looking for thread.

Only the cedar sweetens with age. Cut young
it cries amber sap like bitter tears that
solidify on air. But then it dries its
weeping eyes and lends itself
to the subtlety of saw and plane.
The carpenter's yield
exudes such a patina of time and maturity
it puts me to shame.

So much things to say that might be better
left unsaid.

The pot cannot be made today.
Too much water in the clay.

So much things to say
that lie bitter on the tongue.
You taste the snowflake
I kiss the sun.

NOTES TO THE POEMS

SHELL (2007)

The poems 'Taíno Genesis' (p. 24) and 'The First House' (p. 71) are retellings of the myths of the indigenous Taíno of the Caribbean. 'Cassava/Yuca' (p. 26) also references the cultural practices of the Taíno as does the myth of the sea coming from a broken gourd in 'The Song that it Sings' (p. 34).

'What could be written on a grain of rice' (p. 60) references the indentured Chinese who along with workers from India, were brought to work in the Caribbean sugar cane fields after the enslaved Africans were freed: *Kun-lun* refers to the Daoist earthly paradise.

'Cane piece' in 'Cane Gang' (p.55) refers to the divisions of the sugar cane fields on the plantations.

OVER THE ROOFS OF THE WORLD (2005)

Wild Nester
The words in Italics are songs and sayings from the oral culture of Jamaica and the popular interpretations of bird calls.

Wild Nester – White Belly
The Cockpit Country (also referred to as 'the cockpits' – in 'Blue') refers to a geographical region in Jamaica of eerie and unusual landscape developed in limestone rocks (called by geographers Karst topography).

Penny Reel
Penny reel: dancing round the Maypole, popular in bygone days in the colonies, derived from the European May Day phallic ribbon dance round a pole. In Jamaica, in working class districts where it became a popular social pastime, dancers paid for each 'reel' or turn at plaiting and unplaiting the ribbons round the pole, hence 'penny reel'. 'Penny Reel O' is also the title of a once-popular sexually suggestive folk song.

Ol'Higue: a witch who sheds her skin at night and flies in the shape of a bat to feast on blood. She must assume her skin (and human shape) before daybreak. The term 'Ol'Higue' is also applied to someone perceived as a nag.

Basketmaker
In Warao culture (tropical South America), expert basket makers are believed to have a specially reserved place in the after-life, once they have passed a final post-mortem test of their skills.

GARDENING IN THE TROPICS (1994)

A complete annotation of this book is available online as a PDF: 'Gardening in the Tropics by Olive Senior Annotations to the Poems'.

TALKING OF TREES (1985)

Talking of Trees (p.403)
Parade Gardens now St William Grant Park were laid out in the heart of the city of Kingston in 1870–71 on the 'Parade' which was formerly used by British troops. Over 120 trees including 35 different species – some unique to Jamaica – were

planted out. The gardens suffered many vicissitudes since then and virtually all the trees are gone now but one, Woman's Tongue, who has become a downtown street vagrant – Miss Albizia lebbeck – in her mad way tells their story – and ours. Most of the trees named were once to be found in the park.

Big-tree boys were tough denizens of old-time Kingston who congregated under the Banyan tree.

Seh 'feh!' – a children's game of daring.

Sissoo – (?Dalbergia sissoo) was a rare Indian tree in the park; *su-su* is gossip.

LIST OF ILLUSTRATIONS

p. 17 – 'Botany Corn' (Woodcut from Oviedo's
    Historia Natural Seville, 1535)

p.37 – 'The Unknown Maroon', Haiti
    (Eye Ubiquitous / Alamy)

p.47 – 'Saccharum officinarum – Sugarcane, 1880'
    (Sunny Celeste/Alamy)

p.49 – 'Cane cutter' (Illustration, historic)

p.60 – 'Chinese field workers' (Illustration, historic)

p.65 – 'Beach Hut' (Photograph courtesy of Andreas Oberli)

p.75 – 'Fonthill Abbey' designed for William Beckford
    by the architect James Wyatt (GL Archive/Alamy)

p.78 – 'Louise de Kéroualle', Pierre Mignard
    (Art Collection 4/Alamy)

p.88 – 'The Ruins of Fonthill Abbey', John Buckler, 1825

INDEX OF POEM TITLES

Advice and Devices	298
Albatross	116
Albert Street	385
All Clear, 1928	238
Allspice	123
Amazon Women	283
Anatto and Guinep	258
Ancestral Poem	337
And What of the Headlines?	380
Apartment Life	382
At the Slavery Museum	63
Auction	81
Babalu: Lord of the Earth	315
Bamboo (In Five Variations)	262
Basketmaker	169
Bird-Man / Bird-Woman	170
Birdshooting Season	330
Birth of Islands, The	125
Blue	138
Blue Magic Carpet	142
Brief Lives	269
Cane Gang	55
Canefield Surprised by Emptiness	58
Canoe Ocean	31
Caribbean Basin Initiative	209
Cassava/Yuca	26
Cat's Cradle	208
Childhood	352
Children's Hospital	402
Christmas Pudding	431
City Poem	388

Cockpit Country Dreams   331
Colonial Girls School   353
Colours of Birds, The   275
Concrete City   376
Country Funeral   432
Cropover   374
Cruise Ship Leaving Port at Night   422
Dance of Cranes, The   119
Dead Straight   423
Discovery   124
Dispatcher, The   396
Drought   336
Drought, The   437
Eighth Birthday   347
Embroidery   156
Emperor Penguin   117
Epitaph   364
Eye of Everything, The   440
Eye Wash   412
Eye-Water   413
Eyelet/Aiglet   414
Fabulous Eyelids   411
Fern   251
Finding Your Stone   272
First House, The   71
Fishing in the Waters Where My Dreams Lie   61
Flight   433
Found Poem Regarding Archaeological Concerns   67
Funeral Song   369
Garden Snail   23
Gardening on the Run   293
Gastropoda   15
Gourd   187
Grand-Daughter Learns the Alphabet   428

Green Bush Green Bush Green Bush   426
Green Parakeets   384
Greenhorn   434
Guava   255
Guava Jelly Score   425
Guava/2   256
Guédé: Lord Of The Dead   324
Guinep   257
Hatch   19
Here And There   137
Hill Country   345
Homescape   329
Hook   429
Hummingbird   107
Hurricane Story, 1903   199
Hurricane Story, 1944   204
Hurricane Story, 1951   215
Hurricane Story, 1988   236
Hurricane Watch   420
Hurricanes   32
Illegal Immigrant   224
Immovable Tenant, The   287
Join-the-Dots   68
Killer Bees   417
Knot Garden, The   273
Lacemaker   165
Lady, The   393
Leaving Home   140
Letter from the Lesser World   371
Lost Tropic   141
Lucea Harbour   33
Madam Fate   250
Madman at Traffic Lights   377
Magpie   110

Maize   20
Marassa: Divine Twins   305
Meditation on Red   226
Meditation on Yellow   191
Message in a Bottle   126
Misreading Wallace Stevens   130
Missing   135
Moon   144
Moonshine Dolly   202
Mother, The   391
Mountain Pride   252
My Father's Blue Plantation   270
Nansi 'Tory   355
Nature Studies I   359
Nature Studies II   362
Obatala: Father of Wisdom   306
Ode To Pablo Neruda   171
Ogun: God of Iron   309
Olokun: God of the Deep Ocean   318
One Night, the Father   350
Orunmilla: God of Divination   314
Osanyin: God Of Herbalism   307
Ososi: God of Hunting   308
Ostrich   118
Out/In   415
Oya: Goddess of the Wind   317
Parakeet   109
Pawpaw   261
Peacock Tale, 1   113
Peacock Tale, 2   114
Pearl   28
Pearl Diver   167
Penny Reel   158
Peppercorn   50

Persephone   435
Picture   64
Pineapple   248
Plants   245
Poem Without Ending...   445
Poetics of a West India Dinner Party, The   79
Poltergeist   343
Portrait   348
Prayer   335
Pull of Birds, The   91
Quashie's Song   49
r a i n   386
Reaching My Station   399
Rejected Text for a Tourist Brochure   133
Revelation   365
Riddle   155
S(h)ift   72
Sailor's Valentine   30
Scavenger, The   390
Searching for Grandfather   340
Secret of Capturing Parrot, The   95
Secret of Crusoe's Parrot, The   100
Secret of Flying Close to the Sun, The   98
Secret of Taming Parrot, The   96
Secret of Turning Green Parrot Yellow, The   97
Seeing the Light   280
Send the Fool a Little Further   45
Shango: God of Thunder   311
Shell   70
Shell Blow   39
Shelter   22
Skin   27
Skin of the Earth, The   29
Snail   254

Song of the Cave Valley Man   366
Song of the House   368
Song that it Sings, The   34
Starapple   247
Stowaway   225
Sun and Moon   253
Superficial Reading, A   77
Sure Shot   416
Sweet Bwoy   52
Taíno Genesis   24
Talking of Trees   403
They're Stoning the Mango Tree Again   430
Thirteen Ways of Looking At Blackbird   127
To My Arawak Grandmother   339
To the Madwoman in My Yard   379
Touchstone   342
Tree of Life, The   278
Tropic Love   286
Ultimate Secret, The   103
Victim, The   395
Walking on Eggs   59
'Warning: Keep Away from the Cliffs'   421
West India Cane Piece Rat (1821)   56
What Could Be Written on a Grain of Rice   60
White   162
White Night   418
Wild Nester   145
With My Little Eye...   153
Woodpecker   108
X   358
Yard Fowl   104
Yemoja: Mother of Waters   321